Gaining Ground?

CULTURAL SURVIVAL STUDIES IN ETHNICITY AND CHANGE

Allyn & Bacon

Series Editors, David Maybury-Lewis and Theodore Macdonald, Jr.
Cultural Survival, Inc., Harvard University

Indigenous Peoples, Ethnic Groups, and the State, by David Maybury-Lewis

Malaysia and the "Original People": A Case Study of the Impact of Development on Indigenous Peoples, by Robert Knox Dentan, et al.

Gaining Ground? Evenkis, Land, and Reform in Southeastern Siberia, by Gail A. Fondahl

Ariaal Pastoralists of Kenya: Surviving Drought and Development in Africa's Arid Lands, by Elliot Fratkin

Defending the Land: Sovereignty and Forest Life in James Bay Cree Society, by Ronald Niezen

Forest Dwellers, Forest Protectors: Indigenous Models for International Development, by Richard Reed

Gaining Ground?
Evenkis, Land, and Reform in Southeastern Siberia

Gail A. Fondahl
University of Northern British Columbia

Allyn and Bacon
Boston • London • Toronto • Sydney • Tokyo • Singapore

For Ken and Gwynne

Series Editor: Sarah L. Dunbar
Editor-in-Chief, Social Science: Karen Hanson
Series Editorial Assistant: Elissa V. Schaen
Marketing Manager: Karon Bowers
Consulting Editor: Sylvia Shepard
Manufacturing Buyer: Suzanne Lareau
Cover Administrator: Suzanne Harbison
Cover Designer: Jenny Hart
Editorial-Production Service: Omegatype Typography, Inc.

ISBN: 0-205-27579-6

Printed in the United States of America

10 9 8 7 6 5 4 3 2 1   02 01 00 99 98 97

Royalties from this book are directed to Cultural Survival, Inc., and
the Evenki Cultural Center, Bagdarin, Baunt County.

All photographs are credited to Gail A. Fondahl.

Contents

Foreword to the Series

Cultural Survival is an organization founded in 1972 to defend the human rights of indigenous peoples, who are those, like the Indians of the Americas, who have been dominated and marginalized by peoples different from themselves. Since the states that claim jurisdiction over indigenous peoples consider them aliens and inferiors, they are among the world's most underprivileged minorities, facing a constant threat of physical extermination and cultural annihilation. This is no small matter, for indigenous peoples make up approximately five percent of the world's population. Most of them wish to become successful ethnic minorities, meaning that they be permitted to maintain their own traditions even though they are out of the mainstream in the countries where they live. Indigenous peoples hope therefore for multi-ethnic states that will tolerate diversity in their midst. In this their cause is the cause of ethnic minorities worldwide and is one of the major issues of our times, for the vast majority of states in the world are multi-ethnic. The question is whether states are able to recognize and live peaceably with ethnic differences, or whether they will treat them as an endless source of conflict.

Cultural Survival works to promote multi-ethnic solutions to otherwise conflictive situations. It sponsors research, advocacy, and publications which examine situations of ethnic conflict, especially (but not exclusively) as they affect indigenous peoples, and suggests solutions for them. It also provides technical and legal assistance to indigenous peoples, and organizations.

This series of monographs entitled "The Cultural Survival Studies in Ethnicity and Change" is published in collaboration with Allyn & Bacon (the Simon and Schuster Higher Education Group.) It will focus on problems of ethnicity in the modern world and how they affect the interrelations between indigenous peoples, ethnic groups, and the state. The studies will focus on the situations of ethnic minorities and of indigenous peoples, who are a special kind of ethnic minority, as they try to defend their rights, their resources and their ways of life within modern states. Some of the volumes in the series will deal with general themes, such as ethnic conflict, indigenous rights, socio-economic development, or multiculturalism. These volumes will contain brief case studies to illustrate their general arguments. Meanwhile the series as a whole plans to publish a larger number of books that deal in depth with specific cases. It is our conviction that good case studies are essential for a better understanding of issues that arouse such passion in the world today and this series will provide them. Its emphasis nevertheless will be on relating the particular to the general in the comparative contexts of national or international affairs.

The books in the series will be short, averaging approximately 160 pages in length, and written in a clear and accessible style aimed at students and the general reader. They are intended to clarify issues that are often obscure or misunderstood and that are not treated succinctly elsewhere. It is our hope therefore that they will also prove useful as reference works for scholars and policy makers.

David Maybury-Lewis
Theodore Macdonald, Jr.
Cultural Survival, Inc.
96 Mount Auburn St., 2nd Floor
Cambridge, Massachusetts 02138
(617) 441-5400 fax: (617) 441-5417
e-mail: csinc@cs.org
website: www.cs.org

Preface

Years before that part of Siberia known as Northern Transbaykalia became open to westerners, I became interested in the impact of industrial development on Evenki reindeer husbandry. I had learned a bit of pre-Soviet Evenki life from S. M. Shirokogoroff's 1929 ethnographic classic; a small book entitled *BAM and the Peoples of the North* (Boyko 1979) recounted the challenges facing the Evenki descendants of Shirokogoroff's descriptions, as these peoples witnessed the construction of a railroad (the Baykal-Amur Railroad or BAM) through their homelands. This interest developed into a dissertation topic. To research the effects of the BAM on Evenki reindeer husbandry I spent time in Leningrad, Moscow, and Novosibirsk. I was able to read the archived minutes of early Evenki meetings, as the Bolsheviks created Evenki nomadic councils (the basic level of local administration in the 1920s), to talk to ethnographers who had worked in the region in the 1960s, 1970s, and 1980s, and to read the field notes of some (but not all) of earlier scholars in this region. But I was not able to get to Transbaykalia. Refusals mounted up, on many pretexts, during an academic year spent in Russia, 1987–1988. Finally, in the summer of 1989, weeks before I was to finish the dissertation, I received an invitation from the Chita Institute of Natural Resources. The looming filing date and pregnancy prevented me from accepting.

When, in 1992, I was finally able to visit Northern Transbaykalia, I went to find out more about reindeer herding. (A colleague and expert on reindeer husbandry at one institute in Buryatia recollected receiving a letter from me in 1988 and chortled, "We weren't even allowed to respond to you, a foreigner, this being a closed city. Imagine our state secrets regarding reindeer husbandry!") Evenkis and others politely answered my myriad questions. Vladimir Torgonov, the chairperson of the Baunt County Evenki Association in Northern Buryatia, graciously arranged a visit to two reindeer herds. Reindeer herding was indeed of great concern to the Evenkis, especially given its precipitous decline in recent years. But the conversation always soon turned to land.

By 1992 the Evenkis had actively begun to work toward implementing some of the new legislation that the Soviet, then Russian, federal government had been passing in Moscow. In Baunt County they had achieved some moderate successes—zones of priority Evenki hunting were well on their way to being established, a hunting–herding association appeared to give Evenkis greater control over the products of their labor, and a certain optimism filled the air. Progress in Severo–Baykal County seemed less notable; Evenkis there complained about the inability to receive land allotments for the re-establishment of traditional activities. I had the good fortune of being able to sit in on two land allotment hearings during my short visit to this county, one of which was resolved favorably in my presence. The issue of "land claims" presented a new topic, closely connected to reindeer husbandry. This book recounts my findings over the next few years, as I have tried to sort out what the Evenkis of Northern Transbaykalia have attempted to achieve on the basis of reforming federal and local laws, and what hindrances they have met in their quest to regain some control over their homelands.

ACKNOWLEDGMENTS

The fieldwork required to answer these questions, in a Siberia just recently accessible to foreigners, is still impossible to pursue alone. My work was greatly aided by the Baykal Institute for Rational Nature Use (BIRP), and specifically one of its senior researchers, Darima Mangataeva. I had cited Mangataeva's work on Evenki demography in my dissertation, and was thrilled to be logistically supported by her institute for my first trip. BIRP continued to serve as an academic base, and Darima as my main colleague and traveling companion. With well over a decade of fieldwork in Northern Buryatia, she proved an incredible source of knowledge. As importantly, respect for her was evident in the communities where we worked: people appreciated her willingness to return to the capital (Ulan-Ude) and call about issues they did not seem to be able to resolve locally. As well as a colleague, Darima has become a friend, welcoming me into her family. Her husband, Bair Radnaev, accompanied me to the field when she could not, and provided much other support. A specialist in his own right on transportation infrastructure in Northern Transbaykalia, he also provided much information. Darima and Bair's children Erzhena and Solbon, and their spouses, treated me almost as family (though showing more respect and forbearance than family members are wont). All this made the weeks, and later months, away from home more bearable.

Vladimir Torgonov also deserves special thanks. When I asked in 1992 to be able to visit one outlying village and one reindeer camp, he immediately refused. "No, you must go to two villages—one connected by road [to the county center], one not—to see the difference. You must go to two herding operations, one still under state tutelage, one not, to see the difference." Torgonov repeatedly arranged the logistics of such visits during my several stays in Bagdarin. Visits to the reindeer herding operations became increasingly difficult with skyrocketing fuel costs; Torgonov always managed to find us a way onto a helicopter headed in the general direction of a herd. His wife Nina deserves warm thanks for several home-cooked meals with no assistance, while I plied her husband with questions.

Without the help of other key persons—Darya Mironova, Vladimir Bakumenko, Petr Kalashnikov, Grigory Balkhanov, Alexey and Anna Tochnovy, Petr Mordonov, Alexandra Mordonova, Boris Senchukov, Vladimir Shkarovskiy, Evgeniy Karpov, Valery Zadorozhnyy, Anna Taskerova, Vladimir Renn, Nadezhda Zhumaneeva, Elena

Kurennaya, Evgeniya Polyakova, Mikhail Kozlov, Maria Gabysheva, Nikolay Buyakov, V. N. Vorotnyak, Valentina Nadelyaeva, Natalya Gabysheva-Tokarenko, Svetlana Perfilova, and Victor Ganyugin—fieldwork in Siberia would have been neither as efficient nor as pleasant. The hospitality of some, the advice of others, the arrangements made by yet others, expedited the research. My sincere gratitude extends to Nikolay Kozulin, who afforded me office space in his own small office and access to essential archives while in Bagdarin. Especially heartfelt thanks go to Nikolay Aruneev, Galina Abramova and Galina and Artur Mazholis, for hosting truly incredible working visits, with magnitudes of effort more than I could have ever expected, in each case, on the part of (initially) complete strangers.

I would also like to thank the many Evenkis and other persons, too numerous to mention, who answered my questions patiently and shared their knowledge with me. Discussions and tea with a few individuals must be acknowledged warmly: with Yevdokiya Dogonchina, Nadezhda Sinatorova, Igor Dandeev and Nikolay Naykanchin. I also thank Igor Dandeev, for translating from Evenki to Russian for me during one interview.

Two persons whom I met in 1992, Galina Rogova and Yuri Chernoev, made outstanding efforts in 1994 to show me what they had accomplished in the intervening years. In Rogova's case, this meant finding return transportation across the north tip of Lake Baykal; Chernoev commandeered a tank ("for a smoother ride") to take me ten hours up a forest tract to his land allotment. These, and other, individuals' stories of commitment to reasserting Evenki control over land deserve further attention.

Keeping up with going-ons in Moscow, let alone Transbaykalia, can be difficult from Northern British Columbia. Harald Finkler, Olga Murashko, Gail Osherenko, and Debra Schindler have all provided critical information on legal developments. Kevin Hall has provided opportunities to work on the manuscript by his efficient leadership of UNBC's Geography Programme. Nancy Alexander masterfully and cheerfully drafted the figures under severe time constraints. Greg Poelzer has encouraged this work by his own interest in similar topics of aboriginal self-determination, by critical feedback on earlier drafts of some of the chapters, and by continued collegiality.

The research was supported, at different times, by the National Council for Soviet and Eastern European Research, the International Research and Exchanges Board, the U.S. National Science Foundation and the U.S. National Academy of Sciences. The Institute of Arctic Studies at Dartmouth College, and especially its director, Oran Young, provided much logistical and moral support. Financial support for a visit of four Evenkis and one Buryat to Northern British Columbia in 1995, from the John D. and Catherine T. MacArthur Foundation, allowed me to update some of the information and to discuss land and self-government against a different backdrop of experiences. To all these organizations I am extremely grateful. I also would like to thank Sylvia Shepard of Allyn & Bacon for much help in bringing the manuscript to fruition.

Finally, the deepest thanks are due to my family. My parents Doris and John have provided an environment of intellectual challenge and loving encouragement that led to the career and topics I now pursue. My husband Ken supported many absences from the home front, to Transbaykalia, and to various conferences for presentations on this work. In 1994 he brought our daughter Gwynne, then four, to Transbaykalia for a month, to make a five-month field season palatable. Ken and Gwynne are experts in the geography of playgrounds in Northern Transbaykalia; his care of her and provisioning of our needs allowed me to continue my research while reclaiming family life in the field. Both have been incredibly tolerant of my times away from home, or connected to the computer; both have kept my mood optimistic. Their support and love gives context to this and all of my work.

Land, Resources, and Cultural Survival

In the summer of 1994 M. Y.[1] and I sat in her kitchen and talked. M. Y.'s younger children ran in and out of the back door; her husband stopped to lean against the door frame and lament about the availability of spare parts for farm equipment; her daughter and newborn granddaughter came by to borrow some dinner fixings. A pot of moose stew simmered on the back of the wood-fired stove. We talked of culturally appropriate education, of language, of the demise of traditional handicrafts. M. Y. is an Evenki individual, living in Northern Transbaykalia (in southeast Siberia), who is keenly interested in the culture survival of her people. But mostly, we talked about land.

> I want our clan land, where my ancestors worked and lived, where my parents worked and lived under the *sovkhoz*,[2] where I was born. Not just any

---

1. Names have been abbreviated, and exact dates of interviews not given, to protect the identity of persons interviewed in nonofficial capacities who did not explicitly give their permission to be quoted directly. Unless otherwise indicated, quotes are from author's field notes and interview transcriptions.
2. See Glossary for explanations of Russian and Evenki terms used in the text.

land—I want my native land.... I want it for my grandchildren, not myself. M. Y., June 1994

M. Y.'s words—and actions—capture the essence of a new and vigorous movement among the Evenkis of Northern Transbaykalia. As throughout the world, the Evenkis and other indigenous peoples in the Russian Federation are struggling for rights to their homelands. Dimensions of this struggle include demands for the rights to be able to occupy, use, and govern traditional lands; to steward the resources on these lands in order to ensure their continued availability for future generations; and to protect the homelands from uses that conflict with those supported by and supporting the indigenous population. If only recently commenced, "land claims" demands have progressed rapidly in Russia. M. Y.'s family in the summer of 1994 was in the process of filing a petition which would hopefully result in the land of her ancestors being allotted to her family.

An indigenous individual living in the Russian Federation hardly could have expressed such sentiments as those quoted here even a mere decade before. The Soviet state claimed ownership over essentially all land; to propose indigenous control could have provoked accusations of "bourgeois nationalism" and perhaps even a term in prison. Today, in the throes of radical political and economic restructuring, the Russian Federation is renegotiating land relations as part of its broad palate of reforms. Within a larger framework of land reform, the Russian government has responded to a persistent indigenous lobby by beginning to consider indigenous rights to land. Progress has been tentative—it has engendered in individuals such as M. Y. both hope regarding the nascent federal legislation and despair at its laggard and uneven implementation.

For the Evenkis understands the criticality of land to their cultural survival. Like other indigenous peoples in Russia, over the centuries they developed an identity intimately related to their traditional activities of hunting and reindeer herding—activities which demand extensive land use. In M. Y.'s region of Siberia, the Evenkis refer to themselves as *Orochëny*—the reindeer people (from *oron*, the Evenki word for domesticated reindeer). Two oft-repeated comments summarize many Evenkis' concerns: "Without rights to land there will be no reindeer husbandry," and "Without reindeer, there can be no Evenkis." (e.g., Abramova 1991; Lorgoktoev 1992; fieldnotes 1992, 1994). Without rights to land, and the choice it enables of continuing important cultural activities, the future of the Evenki people is clouded.

THE IMPORTANCE OF LAND

Land, as a resource, is critical to the survival of all humans, a fact many urbanites tend to forget on a day-to-day basis. Those peoples whose survival is more directly linked to land activities develop a special relation to the land, a relation rooted in the depths of their collective history. This special relation to homelands characterizes indigenous peoples throughout the world. For the Evenkis, land provides reindeer forage, supports game species, offers edible and medicinal plants. But land provides more than this: it has symbolic as well as instrumental value (Butz 1996). The Evenki landscape inculcates spiritual meaning, as the homeland of generations past and those to come, and as the earthly nexus between other strata of their cosmology. Place is part of indigenous peoples' collective self-identity. "Much of the life world shared by members of territorially based communities is likely to be bound up in a shared experience of and in that place" (Butz 1996, p. 47).

Today, the most pressing problem facing the Evenki people is the ability to defend their homelands. An influx of nonindigenous population, which envisions Evenki homelands as resource base but shares none of the symbolic valuations which have served to moderate the use of such resources, has threatened the integrity of Evenki lands and the ability of Evenkis to continue to use their lands.

Land lies at the base of cultural identity, political self-determination, and economic autonomy. In essence, land underlies cultural survival. Gaining legal recognition to and protection of their lands—or at least a remainder of these, large and intact enough to support traditional activities in perpetuity—is the key to Evenki future.

INDIGENOUS PEOPLES
OF THE RUSSIAN NORTH

The Evenkis are one of over two dozen distinct peoples (Appendix 1) to whom Russia's northern territories are homelands. These peoples represent a wide range of language families, from Saami (related to Finnish) to Eskimosy (related to the Alaskan Yup'ik) to Nanay (related to Manchurian). They also evince a varied set of adaptations to a zone, which, stretching across 25 degrees of latitude and 160 degrees of longitude, offers a range of environments almost as varied as the peoples themselves. Individual groups and peoples have depended on reindeer herding, hunting and trapping of land and sea mammals, fishing, trade, and, most often, a combination of these activities, to dwell in the North.

The indigenous northerners evolved specific systems of land and resource tenure suited to their environment and integrated with their social structure (Krupnik 1993). Land tenure differed substantially from Western concepts of land ownership. Scholars have only begun to pay attention to, and attempt to understand, the nuances of such differences. Chapter 2 explores our limited knowledge of Evenki relations to their homelands in Northern Transbaykalia, drawing where appropriate on proxy data from neighboring regions.

In the 1920s, Russian ethnographers and policy-makers advanced the concept of a category of "Peoples of the North." Previously, in the early nineteenth century, the Russian state officially recognized non-Russians as falling into three groups, settled, "nomadic" [what today we define as transhumant, i.e., semi-annually changing residence between winter and summer living areas, often connected with animal pastures] and "wandering" [i.e., nomadic, migrating from camp site to camp site throughout the year]. It established a system of colonial administrative relations which formalized this distinction. Most of the peoples living in the northern regions of Russia fell into the last category, of "wanderers," which also included many other of the Russian Empire's encapsulated peoples (see Chapter 3).

In the early years of Bolshevik power, state officials identified the Evenkis as one of twenty-six northern peoples who constituted a distinct ethno-social group, characterized by "extreme backwardness," and needing special attention in order to progress from a retarded stage of development. Pursuing an ideology founded on social Darwinism, officials viewed the peoples of the North stranded in a form of "patriarchal communalism." These peoples would require assistance to skip over intermediate stages of feudalism and capitalism (stages which more advanced peoples in the Russian empire had attained or passed through), to advance toward socialism. The Soviet state pursued a set of policies, at times more concertedly, at times less so, specifically aimed at reshaping the lives of the northern peoples to this purpose. Critical elements of the policy body included sedentarization of nomads, formal education based on a Soviet curriculum, encouragement of part of the population to abandon traditional activities in favor of "Russian" occupations, and annihilation of religious beliefs and many cultural practices (see Chapter 4). Especially critical to this study are the policies of restructuring indigenous relations to the land, through administrative bounding of native lands, through forced relocation of indigenous persons, and through reorganization ("rationalization") of traditional indigenous activities.

If the Evenkis and other peoples who live in the Russian North have been affected by a policy body directed at "civilizing" and "socializing" them, they have no less felt the impacts of other state policies (both Tsarist and Soviet) aimed at expropriating the resources of their homelands. Indigenous homelands in the North include vast tracts of reindeer pasture, hunting and trapping grounds, and fishing waters. They also house much of the minerals, fossil fuels, timber, and furs of the Russian Federation. Resource extraction has decimated large areas of Russia's North, depriving indigenous peoples of the ability to continue the traditional, areally extensive activities of reindeer husbandry and hunting. At the same time, these peoples have seen little, if any, benefit from the extraction of resources (Chapter 4).

In fact, a tragic commonalty among the indigenous northern peoples is that of demographic distress. "All the Northern peoples share one common feature...today, in the 1990s, they live in a situation that can best be described as an 'ethnic catastrophe'" (Vakhtin 1994, p. 31). Infant mortality and general morbidity are high. Life expectancy ran 16–18 years less than the average for Russia as a whole in the 1970s (Pika and Prokhorov 1988); although it improved somewhat over the 1980s, it still fell below 60 years (Pika and Prokhorov 1994).[3] Violent death accounts for thirty percent of all deaths, twelve percent higher than the average for the Russian Federation as a whole. As evident from Appendix 1, several peoples have declined in numbers over one or both of the last two census periods. While the total population of indigenous northerners in North America (Alaska and the Canadian North) has more than doubled in the past three decades (Knapp 1992), in the Russian North it increased by only thirty-eight percent.

Indigenous northerners and Russian scholars attribute this "ethnic catastrophe" in significant part to the loss of control over their homelands and resources. They have underscored the criticality of reestablishing such control to the future of the northern peoples. "The right to manage reindeer pasture and hunting grounds for indigenous peoples of the North is, in essence, the right to survive" (Dmitriev et al. 1990, p. 7). Rights to land and resources dominate indigenous northerners' political agendas.

With the advent of *glasnost* in the mid-1985s, northerners could begin to voice their consternation over the condition of their lives and homelands. Members of the *intelligentsia* of the northern peoples joined together in 1989 to form an Association of the Numerically Small Peoples of the North. This Association has lobbied the government to attend to the problems caused by development strategies which ignored the cultural needs of the northerners, and to reverse a policy characterized at best by poorly informed paternalism, at worst by abject neglect. Faced with this persistent lobby, the Soviet and then Russian government has begun to

---

3. An unconfirmed report gave a life expectancy of less than 35 years for the Evenkis of Severobaykal County and of 38 years for the Evenkis of Baunt County (Belikov and Golubev 1991).

modify its policy toward the indigenous peoples of the North, as witnessed by a growing body of legislation that addresses state-indigenous relations. As demanded by indigenous leaders, much of this legislation focuses on rights to land and resources (Chapters 5–7). Russian Federation legislation adopted since the break-up of the USSR suggests a tentative commitment to strengthening the rights of indigenous peoples, including rights to land and resources. At the same time significant devolution of control over land and resource allocation from central to regional governments poses threats. Indigenous populations constitute numerical minorities throughout the Russian North; a move toward democratic majority rule forebodes decreasing political power for these peoples. Conflicts of interest already are evident, as potential and present foreign investors, domestic entrepreneurs, regional governments, and indigenous groups interpret the evolving body of legislation which guides the reallocation of land and resource.

THE EVENKIS OF NORTHERN TRANSBAYKALIA: A CASE STUDY

A study of the indigenous land reform legislation which has emanated from the governmental chambers of Moscow suggests positive, if so far limited, developments for indigenous rights in the Russian Federation. But have indigenous individuals and collectives savored any of the benefits of these reforms? Too often, studies of policy toward indigenous peoples have focused on the changes at the centers of power, rather than their realization in the peripheries, among the peoples whom they are intended to affect. One intent of this study is to "put a face" on the targets of those policies by examining concrete examples of policy implementation and their reverberations in indigenous communities.

Northern Transbaykalia provides an especially fortuitous context in which to study indigenous land reform for several reasons. Northern Transbaykalia straddles a relatively homogenous tayga (boreal forest) environment, and a relatively homogenous indigenous cultural group, the reindeer herding Evenkis.[4] At the same time, within this region we see a spectrum of industrialization levels. The building of a major railroad across the north of this region challenged Evenki activities along and beyond a corridor of construction. Elsewhere industrial development has been limited for the most part to hearths of gold mining and other mineral extraction efforts. Much of the area remains industrially undeveloped, although affected by proximate nodes of activity. Northern Transbaykalia also straddles two different governmental subunits of the Russian Federation, a republic and a province. Thus the study area allows an examination of how the state bounding of an area affects the implementation of reforms. The Evenkis, divided artificially by political-administrative boundaries imposed by the Soviet state, now experience significantly different successes in their attempts to implement land reform measures, depending on within which set of borders they find themselves encapsulated. Employing a study of one relatively small subgroup of one people in the Russian North also allows for more intimate knowledge of the directions and nuances of land reform at the community level.

Geographical Background

Northern Transbaykalia consists of the three northern counties (*rayony*) each of the Buryat Republic (Severo–Baykal, Muya, and Baunt) and of the Chita Province (Kalar, Tungokochen, and Tungiro–Olyokma) (Figure 1.1). Together they cover some 285.6 thousand square kilometers, about the size of the state of Nevada, and larger than ten of the fifteen former Soviet republics.

Physically, much of the area is either elevated rolling plateaus or mountain range. Peaks reach 2930 m in northeast Transbaykalia, and several of the northern ranges host gla-

---

4. This study does not consider the agricultural Evenkis of the neighboring Barguzin County, and pays only slight attention to the "shore" Evenkis who lived along the northern littoral of Lake Baykal and whose main livelihood was based on fishing and sealing.

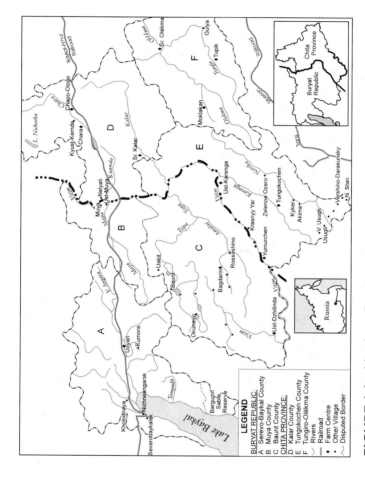

FIGURE 1.1 Northern Transbaykalia.

9

ciers. Alpine tundra—rocky mountain landscapes devoid of trees—predominates at higher altitudes, while tayga, predominantly made up of larch, covers much of the lower elevations. With the exception of a few river valleys and the most southerly extremes, the area does not support agriculture. Widespread reindeer pasture and ubiquitous hunting grounds encouraged the development of an Evenki economy and culture based on game hunting and the keeping of small herds of domesticated reindeer for transport purposes. Some anthropologists identify this area of Eurasia as the hearth of reindeer domestication (Pomishin 1990). Centuries ago, the Evenkis began to hunt furs as a trade commodity; this activity increased in importance over the last three centuries, with the influx of Russians into the area, and with the concommitant heightened articulation with external markets.

Culturally, Northern Transbaykalia is currently home to Evenkis as well as Buryats, Sakha (Yakuts), Russians, Ukrainians, and numerous peoples not indigenous to this part of Siberia. Buryats lived to the south of the Transbaykal Evenkis, but in the nineteenth century moved north, as Russian colonists encroached on their homelands. Sakha groups moved from the northeast into the northern valleys of the Chara and Muya Rivers fairly recently (mid to late seventeenth century). Russians also began to flow into Northern Transbaykalia in greater numbers in the second half of the nineteenth century, especially to the gold-rich lodes of Baunt, first discovered in 1844. These different groups constricted Evenki population distribution. The twentieth century witnessed a huge influx of Russians and other nonindigenous persons, as miners and white-collar workers, especially administrators, dispersed throughout the area. The number of Buryats moving into the northern counties increased substantially as well, especially in the Buryat Republic, but also in Chita Province.

Demographically, the Evenkis, numbering some 2000 individuals, constitute only a small fraction of the population throughout Northern Transbaykalia, from less than one percent in Severo–Baykal County to about fifteen percent in Tungiro–Olëkma County. In the western regions, nonindigenous persons outnumbered Evenkis by the turn of the century—in northern Chita, by the 1930s. By the early 1990s only a few villages remained predominantly Evenki. A large percentage of the nonindigenous population, especially that living in the counties disected by the BAM, is highly migratory; some forty percent of the population in Severo–Baykal County is "temporary," while in Muya County this figure reaches seventy-one percent (Alekseev and Tulokhonov 1993)

Politically the area is divided between a republic and province. Russia consists of a a hierarchy of "ethnic" and "nonethnic" political-administrative units, a legacy of Soviet nationality policy (Kaiser 1994). Fifteen numercially larger peoples within the Soviet state received territorial recognition as Soviet Socialist Republics (e.g., Ukraine, Lithuania, Georgia, Turkmenistan); these Republics have become independent countries. For peoples with fewer members (and peoples not living along a Soviet border), the Soviet government established, in descending order of status, autonomous republics, autonomous provinces (*oblasti*), and autonomous districts (*okrugi*). Fifty-four percent of the territory of Russia (formerly the Russian Soviet Federated Socialist Republic), fell within such "ethnic" units at one or another level; the remainder was carved up into nonethnic territories (*krai*) and provinces. "Ethnic status" assured a certain level of representation in the Council of Nationalities, one of the Soviet Union's two chambers in what was a bi-cameral system of allegedly representative government. It assured the allocation of ear-marked funds for cultural activities of the people recognized, such as newspapers in the native language, means for broadcasting native language programs, and museum funds for expositions related to native culture. Recent legislation has allowed the creation of yet lower levels of ethnic political-administrative territories—"native" counties and "native" townships (Chapter 5).

The Buryat Republic (Buryatia), set up as an autonomous republic in the early 1920s to give territorial recognition to the Buryat people, declared its sovereign status as a constituent republic of the Russian Federation in 1990. Since then it has adopted its own constitution, and its own legal code which parallels, but does not always parrot, the Russian Federation's legal code. Within Buryatia six Evenki Townships and one Evenki County have been established (Chapter 6). Unlike Buryatia, Chita Province does not have any special "ethnic" status, nor do any of its counties or townships. The provincial administration, however, has adopted measures to establish protected areas for Evenki "traditional activities" (reindeer herding, hunting, fishing) based on a creative, if contentious, interpretation of the intent of a (federal) presidential decree. The three counties of the Chita North formerly (1931–1938) constituted the Vitim–Olëkma Evenki National District; some parties advocate the revival of special "ethnic" status for the northern counties in the form of a revived "ethnic" district. Such a district would receive benefits similar to (if at levels less than) that of a republic in terms of recognition of native language and culture, benefits not received by the current "nonethnic" counties of a nonethnic province.

In looking at the implementation of Russian legislation on indigenous rights to land and resources over this politically parceled landscape, we see a number of different approaches being worked out. This variation, in a relatively small, if politically heterogeneous, region suggests the potential for variability for land and resource reform in the Russian North as a whole. Further studies are needed to document developments "on the ground" among other indigenous peoples in other areas of the North (but see Anderson 1995, Grant 1995, and Schindler 1996 for excellent beginnings in this direction).

FIELDWORK: "GROUND-TRUTHING" EVENKI LAND TENURE

Keeping abreast of legislation emanating from the Russian Government allows us to investigate paradigmatic shifts in the landscape of land tenure in the Russian North. Analysis of the recent factual changes in this landscape requires listening to the views of those who are experiencing the effects of legislation passed at a great distance. My analysis of Evenki gains in rights to land is based primarily on interviews with residents of Transbaykalia during 1992–1994. Interviews followed a guided approach, employing a common set of questions but proceeding flexibly to explore issues raised by each person interviewed. Persons interviewed included administration officials at the republican, provincial, county, and village level; presidents of the republican, provincial, county, and village Evenki Associations; former and present chairpersons of *sovkhozy* (state farms), *kolkhozy* (collective farms), *gospromkhozy* (state hunting enterprises), *koopzverpromkhozy* (cooperative hunting enterprises); directors and members of newly created Evenki*obshchinas* ("communes," described in more detail in subsequent chapters), and herding–hunting associations; and former and current hunters, herders, and other indigenous and local persons who are experiencing first hand the changes in land and resource legislation. I also collected spatial information (e.g., boundaries of land allotments, granted and requested) on large-scale topographic sheets (1:500,000 and 1:200,000). Interviewees occasionally provided copies of draft legislation, statistics on traditional economic activities, newspaper clippings on issues related to my research, personal correspondences regarding concerns about land, and advice on other potentially useful interviewees to pursue.

Interviewing in village Siberia depended heavily on a "host," usually an Evenki member of the community, who suggested the interviewees, accompanied me to their homes, introduced my research, and often remained present for the duration of the interview. Sometimes the person also became involved in the questioning and answering. While this system has obvious drawbacks, these are outweighed by the vast advantages to a researcher with limited time in each village. The "host" acted as broker and cultural interpreter (the language of interviews in almost all cases was Russian), and in most cases easily convinced the potential interviewee to dedicate some time to the project (usually one to two hours, occasionally briefer, but sometimes stretching to several hours). We would set out in the morning and proceed, usually unannounced, from door to door, asking for some time, information, answers, stories, and opinions. "Unannounced" did not necessarily mean unanticipated, as word quickly spread that a North American visitor was spending time in the village—an unusual event for villages which had until recently been off limits to foreigners. In most cases we were immediately escorted to the kitchen table. On occasion individuals refused an interview: roughly ten percent of those asked could not, or would not, talk with me. In communities I visited a number of times, I returned, sometimes escorted, sometimes not, to persons I had previously interviewed, and resumed discussions. Group interviews were followed up with individual interviews of the same persons when possible. Requisite to carrying out such field work in village Siberia is the ability to consume copious amounts of tea!

During a month-long visit in 1992, I visited three villages each in Baunt and Severo–Baykal Counties of Buryatia, and flew out briefly to two reindeer-herding camps in Baunt County. A few interviews were conducted at these locations, and also in Buryatia's capital city of Ulan–Ude. A shorter visit (two-and-a-half weeks) in 1993 allowed me to visit Ulan–Ude and the capital village of Baunt County, Bagdarin, again, to travel to Chita, the capital city of Chita Province, to meet indigenous and nonindigenous officials there, and to lay the groundwork for extended work the following year. Both visits served as introduction to a several month field season in 1994 (April–August). While during this period I met with officials in Ulan–Ude and Chita, I spent most of the time in villages (Bagdarin, Ust–Dzhilinda, Rossoshino, Verkh Usugli, Tungokochen, Tupik, Zarechnoe, Staraya Chara, Chapo Ologo, Kyust–Kemda, Nizhneangarsk, Kholodnaya, and Kumora [Figure 1.1]), exploring the impact of the new laws as perceived by the local population. During the 1994 season I also visited one larger herding operation and three remote *obshchina* camps.

Sequential visits over three years allowed a view of the *process* of legal reform, and of reactions to the process over time. They also enabled me to establish a level of rapport with key community members, and a credibility as a committed researcher during a period when, given that the areas just recently had opened to foreigners, many "academic tourists" appeared and disappeared. Access to officials and to official documents improved over time, and second-visit interviews to many individuals provided a wealth of information not offered during initial meetings. Several Evenki individuals I had met in 1992 also took special efforts to show me the fruit of their work in the past two years during the 1994 visit. A 1995 visit by four Evenki village leaders from Northern Transbaykalia to First Nations communities in northern British Columbia allowed further update of information, as has occasional correspondence from heads of two Evenki *obshchinas*.

Fieldwork reveals the views of indigenous persons who benefit—and sometimes suffer from—the legal reforms in Moscow and the provincial or republican capitals. Too often the story of Russia's indigenous peoples, when told at all, has been told from Moscow's vantage. This work attempts to offer alternative interpretations, one "ground truth" of the how reforms play out among the indigenous peoples whom they allegedly attempt to aid, and how indigenous peoples themselves are attempting to force reforms that will truly benefit their ability to survive. The analysis I offered has been influenced by many Transbaykal Evenki individuals with whom I conferred. I thank these persons for sharing unstintingly their time and views, and hope that this small contribution will help make audible some of the voices of those significantly touched by the reforms orchestrated from afar. Of course, this version of the historical and contemporary geography of Evenki land claims is filtered through, and shaped by, my personal experiences and ideals: I also hope that in the near future their voices will be heard more directly by an English-reading audience.

2

Evenki Land Use and Land Tenure

The Evenkis are the most widely distributed of all the Siberian peoples. By the time the Russians began to make contact with them, their homelands stretched from the Putoran Mountains at the base of the Taymyr Peninsula in the North, to China and Mongolia in the South, and from west of the Yenisey River to the shores of the Okhotsk Sea (Appendix 1). Continued expansion took them onto Sakhalin Island in the nineteenth century (Vasilevich 1969). Their homelands cover over one-quarter of Siberia. Numbering 30,163 persons in 1989 (the last Soviet census), they constitute the second largest of the "numerically small peoples of the North" (Pika and Prokhorov 1994).

The identity of the Evenkis as a single people itself is a creation, paradoxically, of the same Russian state-building process which alienated their land (Poelzer 1996). Called Tungus in pre-Soviet times, from the Sakha (Yakut) name for them, *Tongus*, the Evenkis identified themselves by clan: Kindigir, Chilchagir, Turuyagir, and so forth. A common identity as an Evenki people would only be "imagined" and adopted by the Evenkis themselves during the Soviet period (Vasilevich 1969; cf. Anderson 1983). While all belonging to the same Tungusic language (a division of the Tungus–Manchu branch of the Altaic languages), dialects spoken by the Evenkis differed enough as to be unintelligible between some groups. Clans traded, intermarried, and warred with each other, and occasionally coalesced to fight against neighboring peoples. Shamans served as mediators between Evenki lives in this world and in others, higher and lower. Spiritual significance permeated Evenki homelands, invoked in a blending of animism and shamanism. If some sites held special spiritual meaning, symbolic significance pervaded the Evenki landscape as a whole. To come of age was to learn to read this landscape "text," to intimately know and respect one's *place*, to know when and how to propitiate the spirits of the place or to request a shaman's intervention in such a relation.

The Lake Baykal region appears to have been an important hearth of early Evenki culture. Evolving out of the blending of northern and southern aboriginal tribes of Siberia, the Evenki culture shows aspects of both. From around Lake Baykal, Tungus speaking groups moved outward—northwest into the Yenisey watershed, north to the Lena River and its tributaries, and east to the Okhotsk Sea and Amur River, conquering and assimilating other aboriginal peoples (Vasilevich 1969).

Evenki adaptations to the environment in Transbaykalia, and eventually throughout Siberia, involved an extensive use of land. Nomadism allowed this. Harvesting a variety of subsistence resources over large territories enabled the Evenkis (and other indigenous peoples of the Russian North) to reduce their impact on any given area of the sensitive boreal forest. Thinly spread over thousands of square kilometers, the larger Evenki culture begot many regionally specific variations: in some areas hunting dominated, in other areas reindeer herding, in yet others fishing or sealing.

LIFE IN NORTHERN TRANSBAYKALIA: CHANGING GEOGRAPHIC AND SOCIAL RELATIONS

To understand a "typical" life of an Evenki person in northern Transbaykalia, let us take a hypothetical woman,

"Basuk," born around 1900.[1] Basuk was born in a shelter somewhat removed from the camp in which her family and her uncle's family lived. Her mother, going into labor, headed to a special birthing tent, attended by a female relative or two. Basuk was wrapped in soft skins, and laid in a birchbark cradle which was made to strap on the side of a reindeer. Sphagnum moss, absorbent and slightly antiseptic, often served as her diaper. A few days after her birth, she and her mother returned to the family camp, where her older brother and sister danced with delight at their new sister. Two other younger siblings born between her sister and herself, had died: the family tied special amulets above her cradle to ward off evil spirits.

Her early months were spent in the arms of her mother and other relatives, or in the cradle, riding from camp to camp. As Basuk grew older, she began her education—through observation of her older brother and sister, her parents, and relatives. She watched her mother sew clothing, of cotton and tanned deer skins, embellishing them with beads, ribbon, and embroidery. Her mother, a renowned seamstress, also sewed prettily patterned deerskin boots and mittens, which her father took to the Russian trading shop, and traded for tea, flour, and sugar. Sometimes he traded these items directly to local gold miners. Basuk learned how to sew both the cotton that her father brought home from the Russian trading post and the reindeer hides. Eventually she received her own small bag in which she stored her set of hide scrapers and sewing tools. But her real passion was hunting. Her brother showed her how to set traps and how to shoot squirrel, and Basuk eventually brought in many. The other girls might laugh at her "boyish" ways, while they sat and sewed their fine reindeer *kumalany*, but she felt proud of her ability to provide extra trading goods for the family's trips to the local trading post.

---

1. This imaginary Evenki's life merges details of the lives of many women with whom I conversed between 1992 and 1994. It is not representative of any single life, but rather meant to be suggestive of the various events common to an Evenki person living in Transbaykalia during this period.

Ksenya Kutonchina with a *Kumalan*
(reindeer skin patchwork).

When her father returned home from these visits to the
Russian's post, he always brought some candy for the kids.
Basuk's mother would unpack the bags, take the flour out,
make some flatbread, and boil some tea. They would all sit
around the fire and enjoy the tea, sweetened with sugar. Although the sugar would soon be gone, the family often ate
flatbread with their boiled moose or elk meat, and always
drank tea. In the summer, Basuk loved to gather berries and
mix them with the thick creamy reindeer milk for a real
treat. The milk also "whitened" the tea, once the sugar was
used up.

One of Basuk's favorite jobs was to watch over the reindeer calves each spring. She and her sister would tie them
up near their tent. When the cows returned to nurse the
young reindeer, they would call their mother, who would
milk each deer before she let it suckle its young. Basuk also
enjoyed the tangible excitement of breaking camp—packing

the family's belongings on the back of the deer, agreeing to meet their father in a day or two's time at a new site, and heading along the forest trail. The deer caravan, with a sacred white reindeer in the lead, looked so picturesque, and when Basuk tired of walking she could sit astride one of the riding reindeer. A new camp, a new view—often vaguely familiar from last year or the year before—offered untold opportunities for exploration and discovery. In the winter she strapped on her skis, donned her hat with its long, long earflaps, and set out over the snow, sometimes behind the deer, sometimes ahead. She enjoyed the long winter nights, snuggled in her sleeping bag, listening to her grandmother tell riddles and stories.

Basuk's occasional childhood illnesses were treated with medicines processed from local herbs. Her mother gathered different plants from various sites in their territory—some from the alpine meadows, other from the forest. At one point her cousin badly burned her hand, too badly to be treated by any of these medicinal plants. The family had recently given up its reindeer hide tent for a canvas one, heated by a small iron stove, which the young child had backed into. Luckily a local shaman had been nomadizing nearby. He treated the burn with a bear-paw, which covered the niece's hand for a day and a night. When he removed it, what had appeared to be a nasty scorch left almost no scar.

Once a year the camp members—her family, her grandparents, her aunt and uncle, and her cousins—headed to the shore of Lake Baunt, near the little Russian church, where the annual fair convened. Here they met with dozens, sometimes hundreds of other Evenki families. What a time! Visiting, dancing, exchanging gossip rich in information. The adults compared herd size growth, the condition of pastures, the visitations of disease to human and herds. They traded reindeer bulls, for "freshening" of the herds' blood. Youngsters played. Circle dances and story telling by elders continued deep into the night, and reconvened the following evening. Basuk looked forward for weeks to these meetings. But by the end of the fair, she was secretly happy to return to the quiet life of her camp. In the summer the members of her own camp might join with another family or two for short periods—also a nice change of pace, with new stories and new riddles to be shared. Life was rarely dull.

Basuk's family owned about 30 reindeer—she herself had received two at birth, and by the time she was ten had several more, the offspring of these deer. But in 1912 an epizootic (animal epidemic) hit, killing all but nine reindeer of her family's herd. Life became much more difficult for several years after this. Her brother, now in his late teens, went to a gold mine, not far from the southern part of Basuk's family's hunting territory, and there worked as a hay cutter. He even tried his hand at panning gold. For a few years Basuk's father hired out to a distant relative whose herds had not been decimated, and helped herd his deer. Basuk and her mother spent more time sewing goods for trade. Meat was scarce, and Basuk grew thin. Things were worse for other families, who found few live wild deer to hunt; two young nephews died, their mothers unable to produce enough milk to feed them.

By the time Basuk was in her mid-teens, the family's herd had grown to its previous size, and life was again easier. Her mother and father began to discuss marriage. One year, at the annual fair, they spent a considerable amount of time talking with others, especially elders. Toward the end of the gathering they announced that they had found a suitable husband, Tyan. From another clan, his family was not rich in deer but had a moderate herd. Tyan himself was well known as a skilled hunter. Basuk, while shy about the thought of meeting and marrying a man she had only met a few times at the annual gatherings, was glad that her parents had been able to arrange such a good match. Folks sometimes called Tyan Mikhail; his birth had been registered at the small Russian Church on the shores of Lake Baunt, and the Russian minister had insisted on a Russian name.

Tyan came several months later to work for Basuk's father. Basuk soon confirmed her first impressions; Tyan was a dedicated herder and skilled hunter. When the day came, months later, for Basuk to leave her family and go to live with Tyan's family, Tyan having served his agreed-upon term of labor in exchange for her hand in marriage, she did so with few misgivings, if with a sadness that the rivers and hills she knew so well would no longer be her home. She looked forward to the next annual fair where she would see her family again.

Basuk soon gave birth to her first child. In the cold of March she headed out to the flimsy shelter, to shiver between contractions. Her labor was a difficult one, and later her mother-in-law told her how the people back in camp had been instructed to undo knots to help her travail. When her bleeding wouldn't stop at first, a shaman was sent for. She prepared concoctions from her medicinal herb chest, requiring Basuk to drink some and applying others topically. It took Basuk several weeks to recuperate, but Tyan and Basuk's mother-in-law helped care for Anna, a large, robust baby. Basuk's mother-in-law had wanted to name the child Gurchen, after a recently deceased relative, but Basuk and Tyan thought a Russian name had a more modern ring. Each year brought more contact with Russians.

In fact, the following year, an unpleasant side of this contact emerged. Tyan returned to camp from a few days' hunt with a sable and a tale of how a neighboring Evenki family had lost most of its deer to marauding Russians. The Russians said that they were soldiers and they needed the deer for meat. There was talk of a revolution, whatever that was, and of "red" people and "white" people.[2] Tyan had noticed other hints of such unrest; the Russian who ran the trading post he usually frequented had intimated that he might not be around long. Tyan thought it might be better were he replaced; terms of trade seemed to ever worsen, and during the last few visits rifles and ammunition had been in short supply.

By the time Anna was six, she had a little brother, Petr (Basuk had lost her second child only a week after its birth). Basuk and Tyan worked hard; they had faced another loss of several reindeer to another disease, but the herd was back to

---

2. Following the Bolshevik Revolution, Russia experienced a several year civil war, in which the Communists ("Reds') fought against a number of opposition parties, often collectively referred to as "Whites."

forty deer now. They worried about the future of their children, as more and more Russians seemed to be appearing, wanting to hunt the lands of their neighbors, and showing little respect for many of their customs. On the other hand, things had improved at the trading center. Someone named "Soviet" seemed to be running it; prices had decreased, and he was offering better terms of trade for the pelts that Tyan and Basuk trapped. Guns were still hard to come by. Once, when Tyan had wanted to choose more goods than he had pelts, in order to bring some treats home for Basuk and Anna, this Mr. Soviet had offered to extend credit. Tyan was hesitant, but agreed. He was delighted to find on his next trip, that the trader kept his word about the agreed-upon terms. The former trader often changed his.

When Anna was almost a teenager, Tyan and Basuk were visited by a man who explained that Soviet power ruled, and that they should join a collective. Tyan and Basuk had a hard time making out where this fellow was coming from; he seemed pleasant enough and brought tea and candy. He also brought several pamphlets with red print, which he said he wanted them to be able to read. Tyan knew how to sign his name; this man said they should both attend literacy school. He also asked if Basuk, Tyan, Tyan's family (father and mother, and older brother and his family), with whom they nomadized would collectivize. When it turned out that all he wanted was for them to continue doing what they had always done, but call themselves the "Sable Collective," they saw little harm and agreed.

Much more disturbing was the day when this man appeared again and told them that Petr should go to school. School, it turned out, was one of those Russian buildings in the Russian village some kilometers away. The village had originally only had a few Russians in it, including the man who ran the trading post; lately a few Evenki families seemed to be spending increasing amounts of time. Petr would learn to read, the man said, and would be taken care of—fed and clothed—during his time away from home. Basuk and Tyan protested; Petr was just learning to lay traps and use a rifle well, and promised to be a skilled hunter, if his interest in reindeer husbandry was less marked. Eventually they managed to dissuade the man from taking Petr, but he promised to be back before the end of the summer.

This hypothetical life of one Evenki person provides a brief summary of the livelihood of Transbaykal Evenkis, some of the "traditional" elements of their lives, the challenges facing them from time immemorial, and new and distinct challenges arising in the final years of the Tsarist period and first decades of the Soviet period. Chapters 3 and 4 offer more detail on these challenges and Evenki responses to them. In the remainder of this chapter, we leave the imaginary Basuk to look at the two most important activities for Evenki livelihood, and the spatial organization of these activities.

EVENKI HERDING AND HUNTING IN NORTHERN TRANSBAYKALIA

Using a wide spectrum of local resources, which varied temporally and spatially, the Evenkis of Transbaykalia relied for their livelihood on an integrated set of activities.

> My father was a hunter. In the summer he cut hay and collected berries with his son. In the winter we hunted for fur and meat and caught fish. In the spring and summer we dried meat and rendered fat. Father traded furs and meat for flour, hunting guns, and so forth.
>
> We stored flour and tea on a *labaz* [elevated storage platform]. In the winter our tents were of hide, in the summer of birch. Father knew how to speak Russian, our brother spoke Chinese. Mother worked hides with the older daughter. There were eleven of us: five brothers, six sisters. They taught the kids how to do all this. (Glazirova 1990)

Reindeer herding, hunting, trapping, fishing and trading with neighboring and distant peoples constituted the main "economic" activities; other pursuits rounded out this palate. On the north shore of Lake Baykal, sealing also contributed to the seasonal round. It is worth underscoring that while outsiders often identify these activities as "economic," they also

fostered social relations, cemented kinship ties, often contributed to spiritual life—to view them as simply economic activities is to oversimplify and even denigrate their importance to all facets of Evenki culture and cultural persistence.
After the coming of Russians, short-term contract labor (e.g., cutting hay) became yet another option to pursue. The effort put into one activity over others depended on season, environmental conditions, potential for trade with other peoples, personal preference, and talents. By relying on greater or lesser dependence on different activities Evenkis enjoyed a great flexibility in meeting their physical and spiritual needs.
Two activities, however, stand out in Evenki culture and self-identity: reindeer herding and hunting.

I want to say, what an important role hunting and reindeer herding had for the indigenous population. Our ancestors, our parents lived by the tayga, raised their children, and didn't know what a potato or a coupon was. They could get meat and fish and clothing, not from the store, but produced by themselves, which is priceless these days. Because it is soft, yet strong, warm and comfortable, and it is almost impossible to get now. (Chekundaev 1990)

As mentioned in Chapter 1, many of the Evenkis of Transbaykalia called themselves "reindeer people" (*Orochëny*). Prior to the Soviet period, families kept relatively small herds, ranging from a few dozen to a few hundred animals. Unlike the large-scale "carnivorous pastoralism" (Ingold 1980) practiced by Siberian peoples of the tundra, wherein the main product of reindeer husbandry was meat and herds numbered in the thousands of animals, the Evenkis and neighboring tayga herders kept their animals mainly for transport and milking. Reindeer were culled for meat for ritual purposes, in times of need, and when it was apparent that the animal would not survive another season. For the most part, Evenkis depended on wild game for their meat, and their own animals for mobility and milk.
Reindeer allowed the Evenkis to move through the boreal forest in search of game and furs. Well adapted to moving

through snow and swamps, along narrow paths and across scree slopes, feeding both summer and winter on vegetation underfoot, and living year round outside, without need for barn or shed, reindeer provide a means of mobility unmatched by any other animal in tayga conditions. Astride their reindeer, Evenki hunters could cover large territories in search of fur-bearing animals, on which was based the largest part of the Evenki barter and monetary economy. On backs of reindeer, tents and provisions, furs, and children were transported from camp to camp. Reindeer also provided skins for clothing, housing and other needs, tendons for thread, antler and hooves for glue, antler and bones for buttons, flatware handles, pipes, saddle pommels, and a variety of other domestic implements. Outerwear and tents made from reindeer hides remain unsurpassed in terms of heat retention.

The nomadism of reindeer breeders (and other pastoralists) is frequently seen as a strategy of exigency. Those who can't afford to settle, due to a combination of environmental conditions and a dearth of adaptive skills to these, are forced to migrate with their animals. Reindeer demand movement over substantial territories, in order to find, and not overgraze, forage. Thus, from a Western point of view, peoples such as the Evenkis are relegated to a life of incessant movement—a negative feature indeed. Yet, among the Evenkis those individuals who had lost their deer and thus had been forced to settle were viewed as much worse off than the nomadic *Orochëny*. The settled were characterized as a people "paralyzed by the dream of distant mountains" (Tugolukov 1980, p. 67, quoting Pokrovskiy), who, "completely paupered, drag out the most miserable existence [and] crave deer, so that they can return anew to be *Orochëny*, i.e., nomads" (Neupokoev 1928; cf. Grigorovskiy 1890).

Nomadism, which reindeer husbandry allowed, provided the Evenkis' ultimate link with their homelands, with tenure of the tayga and alpine tundra, valley and summit, swamp, and uplands. One outsider elegantly observed that "migration is the poetry of the Tungus" (Tugolukov 1980, p. 66). This aesthetic of nomadism is also mirrored in the words of a Transbaykal Evenki, A. Komaritsyn: "To feel the beauty and charm of nature is possible only when a smoking tent and pasturing deer are nearby..." (quoted in Tugolukov 1980, p. 66).

Transbaykal reindeer husbandry differed from that of other areas of Siberia in one important dimension. Throughout much of northern Transbaykalia, the women dominated herding activities during the better part of each year. Men left the camp to hunt for meat and furs; women gathered the herds, broke camp, moved the family's provisions to a new site, and set up the new camp. Women also milked the deer and tamed the young. Disregard on the part of state officials for this distinctive pattern has been, according to some Evenkis, a key factor in the decline of reindeer herds over the last several decades (see Chapter 4).

Reindeer herding, Evenki-style, was not especially labor intensive; in fact, the concept of herding as a "profession" prior to the Soviet period is anachronistic: "one might say that in the tayga there are no reindeer herders, but rather hunters with reindeer" (Pika and Prokhorov 1994, p. 98). Reindeer required limited attention during much of the year. Human-reindeer interactions were continuous but not demanding, except for short periods during calving and mating seasons.

In the spring, the Evenkis moved their "smoking tents" to south-facing slopes of the valleys, where the snow melts first, or into the forests, where it remains friable. They camped in these areas as they migrated with their herds to the reindeer's traditional calving grounds. During the calving, reindeer cows were watched continuously, as reindeer about to give birth might try to leave the herd, and newborn calves were easy targets for predators. Early human contact with calves helped the domestication process. After calving, those camps which had a moderate number of reindeer headed to rivers, to hunt for the moose and wild reindeer which would be browsing the new growth. When a kill was made, especially of a moose, the camp would be relocated to the site of the kill. Women took over the tasks of butchering and preparing the meat for storage, men would reconvene the hunt. By June, elk would also be hunted for their valuable velvet antlers. As the weather grew warmer, Evenki families might exchange their reindeer- and moose-hide tents for ones covered with birch-bark.

As summer set in, Evenki families rich in reindeer drove their herds to alpine pastures, where they hunted for musk-deer and marmot. Here, with the help of mountain breezes and lingering snow fields, the deer enjoyed a relatively in-sect-free existence, and were thus more easily kept together. Evenkis remaining in the tayga used smudge fires to protect their herds from the mosquitoes and biting flies that could drive the animals wild. By mid-summer, when the lichens began to parch and insects somewhat abated, the herding groups would disperse from the mountains, heading for the river valleys. Here they would join in the hunt for large game. Summer migrations were frequent, in order to evade insects, to protect pasture from trampling, and for hygiene. Long stationary periods led not only to pasture degrada-tion, but to the infestation of the camp with warble fly lar-vae, one of the banes of a reindeer's existence.

The poorest Evenkis, those with too few deer to support such migrations and hunting, hired on as herders with richer Evenkis, or spent the summers along rivers and lakes, de-pending to a greater extent on fishing. Children of all fami-lies learned the needed mix of skills of herding, fishing, processing foods and hides, and manufacturing items, main-ly by observation. One bad season could wipe out the stock of a rich herding family, forcing on its members to a depen-dence on fishing and hunting. Fast growth of herds allowed rapid recovery of status to those with talent.

For children, thus, it was important to attain a level of competence in all of the activities which constituted the Evenki spectrum of livelihood. Yet, while instruction in all fields began early, comprehensive responsibility for the com-plex of activities required of one's gender came only with adulthood. Evenki children in families rich and poor enjoyed a relatively lengthy childhood, with slow assumption of obli-gations. Children were encouraged to develop the skills for which they had a special proficiency (Strakach 1962). Gender roles defined as normal certain activities for women and men. Women were expected to tend camp and young children, keep the fire, prepare the meals, sew, milk and tend the reindeer. Men hunted, trapped, made many of the larger tools and weapons, and participated in seasonally intensive activities related to reindeer breeding such as castration, sawing off of antlers, and overseeing the cows during calving. These gendered categories of work proved, however, permeable; for instance, not infrequently did girls seriously pursue hunting as a passion. Girls and boys alike might follow a spiritual calling to skills of a shaman.

At the end of the summer, Evenki groups would head to trading posts to stock up on supplies needed for the fall-winter hunt. Summer supplies would be cached in the *labazy*, elevated storage platforms, and winter supplies retrieved from these. Labazy were located strategically along routes of migration and stocked with foodstuffs, matches, kindling, and other critical supplies. Any person in need could borrow from these, with the expectation that he or she would restock the labaz when possible.

Tulbukonov's *Labaz*.

Rutting season preceded the winter hunt. Herders select-ed the best young bulls for studs, and castrated the rest. They sawed off the antlers of the bulls to prevent injury dur-ing courting fights. The rut posed many dangers. Wild rein-deer bulls would descend on the herds to recruit cows at great loss to the herders. They would engage in fights with the bulls. Domestic bulls would also try to separate a "har-em" from the herd, and drive it off some distance from the camp to protect it from other bulls in the herd, which in-creased the chance of losing cows to predators or wild bulls. Mushrooms, a delicacy for which the reindeer would forage greedily, further exacerbated a herder's task of keeping the herds together during this busiest herding period.

In the late autumn, Evenki families returned to rivers, along which they began to hunt for fur-bearing animals. These animals' pelts were only valuable if hunted during the cold season. With the onset of the most frigid and dark-est period (mid-December to mid-January), hunting activity slowed, and migrations ceased. After the penetration of Russians, mid-winter was marked by the major social event of the year, a big trade fair. Evenkis congregated to trade the season's harvest, to resupply themselves with ammunition and purchased foodstuffs, to pay taxes, and to visit with each other. During these festivals betrothals were arranged, marriages scheduled, and information exchanged regarding all matters. The mid-winter gatherings offered opportuni-ties for long hours of story telling and the recounting of oral histories. Those suffering from maladies might use these op-portunities to consult with shamans from other regions.

Hunting and supervision of traplines picked up again in late January until March. Another trade fair toward the end of March signaled the end of the fur hunt. Large game—moose, elk, and wild reindeer—became the target of the hunt, pursued on skis. Camps favored sites near ravines and depressions, where the snow had accumulated, and where hunters on skis enjoyed an advantage of mobility over the wild deer, elk, and moose, which now broke through the snow's crust. During April, the Evenkis once more headed to traditional calving grounds.

Reindeer provided the mobility that allowed hunters to maximize their harvest within the constraint of strict codes of hunting behavior. Prohibitions existed (and continue to exist) against excessive harvesting of any animal and the killing of certain animals in certain seasons, and the taking of some at any time. Tradition prescribed specific means of killing animals, and the disposition of their bones and other remains. By following these rules, the Evenkis ensured a continued favorable relation with the spirits of the animals and their keepers.

Hunting provided not only as sustenance, and confirmed spiritual ties between animals and humans, but nourished social relations as well. The Evenki practice of *nimat* required that any animal harvested be shared among all members of the nomadic camp. The skin was given to a member of the hunter's mother's clan. More intricate rules surrounded the disposition of a young man's first kill of each species. Even after the commercialization of hunting and imposition of taxes payable in furs, skins of nonfur animals and all meat remained subject to the practice of *nimat*. Reindeer themselves escaped commercialization within Evenki society; deer could be gifted but not sold to other Evenkis (Vasilevich 1969).

Hunting and herding were inextricably linked—having too few reindeer meant poor mobility and poor harvests. Rich herders, on the other hand, had less time to spend on hunting, and less need for the income it provided. Given that one's reindeer could easily succumb to predators or disease, Evenkis depended on the ability to flexibly balance the mix of activities at any time.

EVENKI LAND TENURE

Herding, hunting, and other activities were carried out communally, by the basic unit of Evenki society, the *obshchina*. This flexible association of members of a single extended family or a few families nomadized together. In earlier centuries it appears that obshchinas usually formed from men of a single clan, Evenki society being patrilineal and patrilocal (i.e., children were born into their father's clan, and a women upon marriage took up residence with her husband's family, relocating to his clan territory). Later, with migrations and relocation provoked by Russian encroachment on Evenki territory, and the ravages of introduced disease on clan composition, obshchinas often came to incorporate more than one clan. Ethnographers see the obshchina taking precedence over the clan as the fundamental unit of organization by the latter Tsarist period (cf. Shirokogoroff 1966; Vasilevich 1969). The obshchina owned property collectively: the fire, flint and hook for hanging the cooking kettle, some of the reindeer (some were owned by individuals), the storage platforms (*labazy*). It also enjoyed collective rights to a given territory. Each obshchina had its own "rivers," a watershed or watersheds in which it traditionally hunted and herded.

Yet ethnographic accounts note that others could seemingly use these territories as well; one Transbaykal Evenki alluded to the flexibility of ownership:

> When [hunters] gather together to hunt for squirrel, they agree among themselves on what river to hunt squirrels, but in any event, don't necessarily hunt on that river, but where there are many squirrels. For the hunting of other animals, there are no agreements whatsoever—they hunt where they wish. (Abramov 1930)

The boundaries of an obshchina's land seem exceedingly permeable, and Evenki rights to these territories very flimsy, to the Western observer. What was the nature of "ownership" over obshchina territories?

If Western cultures have imbued nomadism with a false sense of desperation, they have also invested land with commercial value, regarding it as a marketable commodity. Land can be bought, sold, and owned. Attachment to land varies greatly; long time residents of a region, especially those involved in land-based activities such as agriculture, often experience ties that extend beyond viewing their land simply as a material possession. The great mobility, however, for a large sector of Western society, has severed intimate ties to place of birth (and birth of one's ancestors). This has led to a situation where one parcel of land may easily replace another, if its material attributes are roughly the same. Indigenous peoples throughout the Russian North, including the Evenkis, have viewed the lands on which they and their ancestors have lived—their homelands—in a radically different way. Land, its features, and its inhabitants (animate and inanimate) are to be "known" (Anderson 1995). Intimate knowledge of the land, coupled with requisite respect for the spirits of the place and beings which they inhabit (animal, plants, rocks, etc.) entitle indigenous obshchinas to use the land and its resources. This knowledge and familiarity constitutes the core of Evenki territorial tenure. It differs so fundamentally from Western bases of land ownership that Westerners commonly failed to recognize *any* form of indigenous tenure over land among the Evenkis and other northern nomadic peoples:

> The place where one was born and grew up, is called the homeland of that person, and each holds it dear, respects it and loves it. The Tungus [Evenki] has no homeland because all of his life he spends in uninterrupted movement from one place to another …thus he doesn't remember the real place of his birth, he doesn't care about it, he doesn't even ask his relatives about this—in one word, he has no homeland and is not tied to any locale, but like an animal strays the uninhabited deserts or taygas: that is his element. (Orlov 1858)

Such passages afford us information on Western stereotypes of indigenous land tenure, not on tenure systems themselves. Rather, if Evenkis "wandered" the tayga, hunting and pasturing their deer, they did so through a set of discrete (if extensive) plots of the tayga. Members of an obshchina exploited the same territory over several generations. Each new generation developed a familiarity with the land's material and nonmaterial attributes; each generation came to know, through habitation, study, and use, an areally extensive place. Each Evenki generation became, in time, a part of that place.

Evenkis psychologically identify themselves with a home, conceiving of it not in the form of an abstract *chum* [tipi-style tent] in an abstract place, but in the form of that tayga territory where their hunting, pasturing, and fishing grounds, with the material objects of subsistence, are located, calling this territory "my land," "home." (Sirina 1992a, p. 80)

Even after seven decades of Soviet rule which challenged Evenki tenure, often removed families from their traditional territories, or hindered their attempts to use the land (Chapter 4), "Evenkis themselves with more or less confidence name of rivers and areas of the tayga belonging to them, where the migration routes of their families and neighbors were" (Turov 1990, p. 133). They clearly differentiated between their own and "other's" territory. As M. Y. said, "Not just any land—I want *my native land*" (M. Y., June 1994; see Chapter 1).

Extreme events, such as severe fires (and the subsequent lengthy time required for the regeneration of reindeer lichens), mass death of deer, or human epidemic might dispossess an obshchina of its priority use of territory, as others moved in to utilize the unused pasture and hunting grounds. But under normal conditions, tenure was tenacious; a nomadic existence in no way could be equated with the lack of ties to the land. "The Evenkis held dearly and protected their lands," asserted an Evenki historian from Northern Buryatia (Shubin 1967, p. 95).

Rights to the use of resources on this territory, and rights to exclude others from such use, flowing from membership in an obshchina, were variegated. The obshchina's members enjoyed exclusive rights to some of its territory's resources. Other resources (e.g., certain game species) in the territory might be used by nonmembers only with permission. "Outsiders" enjoyed free access to some sites and their resources, such as fishing sites and pasture resources during migrations. Flexibility and incomplete dominance characterized the Evenki land tenure system. A more perceptive observer than Orlov (quoted previously), A. Mordvinov captured a few of these facets of land-tenure flexibility in his description of Evenki land tenure in the mid-nineteenth century:

> Many of the places comprising the nomadic lands of the Orochëny, as a result of ancient agreements, are divided between them, in some way, into separate allotments, which are known, either by orally transmitted means, or by some kind of sign.... Thus each family or several together have one general allotment, as inviolable property, where they may hunt freely, and if it happens that, going along the boundaries of their allotment the Orochën notes that there is sable, fox, squirrel or marten only on another's side, he may track it, but having killed it only use the meat, the skin is given to the "owner" of that allotment, where the animal was killed. However, in such conditions, when a predatory animal—a bear or wolf—is chased, even through two or three others' allotments, the hunter has the right to use the skin too, as a reward for shooting a hostile neighbor, and moreover, to receive yet additional thanks from the host of that allotment, who has been delivered from a dangerous visitor. (Mordvinov 1851, p. 129)

Our very lack of understanding of such nuances of land tenure has prevented us from even asking discerning questions about such indigenous land tenure systems until recently. Too often it has given rise to Western perceptions of indigenous lands as commons open to all, rather than communal property with a complicated—and markedly flexible—system of access and use rules of those not belonging to the "commune." Moreover, the politics of the former Soviet Union severely problematized any inquiry into indigenous land "ownership". Only now are scholars beginning to examine the multidimensionality of indigenous land tenure (see Sirina 1992a,b, 1995; Turov 1990).

Indeed, the obshchina territories themselves were, in the end, not inalienable. Among the Evenkis, clan elders could, under certain circumstances, redistribute obshchina territories (Shirokogoroff 1966) for the benefit of other clan members:

> The distribution of territory among families is still a clan function... the granting of hunting or pasturage rights—the actual use of territory—to other clans is also a clan affair. So there are two kinds of territory in use: territory used by...a family or families—for hunting, pasturage of reindeer, hay and pasturage of horses, which is either distributed by the clan or occupied by the people who need it; and territory used by the clan for nomadizing, hunting, and fishing of the whole unit, the latter being distributed by the clan among clan members. (Shirokogoroff 1966, p. 295)

Yet we return to the sense of "knowing" a place; one's own territory was familiar both in the physical sense, and regarding the forces or spirits which populated it. Activities on others' territory arose a level of discomfort, due to the alien nature of the place's forces (Turov 1990). Connected with a place, Evenkis sought to nurture this connection, and respected the connections of others to their own places, while practicing a flexibility that enabled cultural persistence in severe tayga conditions.[3]

---

3. Almost no work has been done to date on the gender dimensions of indigenous land tenure in the Russian North. Among the Evenki and many other groups, a man might spend a year or two with his future wife's family, working in their territory. The woman, once married, often moved to her husband's family's territory. The tensions and accommodations involved in living and working in a place which was not "known" would be a fascinating avenue for future research into the dimensions of indigenous land tenure.

3

Losing Control: Alienation of Evenki Land During the Tsarist Era

Russian[1] colonists began to encroach on Evenki lands in the mid 1600s. Having conquered the centralized khanates of southwestern Siberia at the end of the 1500s, they spread eastward to the Pacific Ocean by 1640, a drive inspired largely by a quest for furs. Rapidly overexploiting the more easily accessible valleys of Siberia's largest rivers, fur traders turned to their tributaries to find new lands and indigenous hunters who could furnish them with "soft gold."

Why the rush for furs? The trade in "soft gold" for centuries played a critical role in contributing to the state coffers (Martin 1986). As early the late 1600s value of furs extracted from Siberia equaled about ten percent of the state's income, at Moscow prices. They were sold at markedly higher prices abroad (Forsyth 1992), supplying the nobility of Europe and the Middle East.

---

1. "Russian" will be used here and in the following chapters as a shorthand for the people not indigenous to the north of the Russian empire and later the Soviet Union. While ethnic Russians predominated, Ukrainians, Tatars, Poles, and other ethnic groups came to the North in significant numbers.

Most valuable of all furs was the sable. Even when Canada began to provide rich furs to Europe, the absence of this animal in the Western Hemisphere ensured the continued importance of Siberia in the world's fur markets. The Evenkis of Transbaykalia shared their homeland with the most valuable of the sable subspecies, the dark Barguzin sable.

Knowing the land and being skilled hunters, the indigenous population provided the best means of supplying the state with such wealth. To this end, as the Russian Empire expanded, it imposed a tribute, the *yasak,* on all of its Siberian "subjects." Male natives were required to make an annual payment of a certain number of furs. To ensure the delivery of this crucial treasure, the state forced native leaders to take oaths guaranteeing payment, and frequently took hostages from among the clan leaders. At the same time, those clans which submitted to the yasak payments were promised protection against extortion by other traders. Yet local officials and private traders often levied tribute much higher than that specified by the Tsar, pocketing the difference.

Some native groups willingly agreed to become subjects, as the Russians, with their superior weapons, could provide them protection against neighboring tribes who were hostile. Others resisted, either by armed combat, or by evasion. It was the fierce resistance of the Buryat people, living to the south and east of Lake Baykal, which set Russians around the north end of Lake Baykal in their quest for new fur sources. The Evenki population of Northern Transbaykalia, smaller and more dispersed than the Buryats, offered less opposition (Atlas Zabaykal'ya 1967). By the late 1600s, the Russians had constructed a network of trading posts and wintering huts, from which to exact tribute, control trade, and extract the valuable furs from this area (Figure 3.1).

STATE POLICY
TOWARD INDIGENOUS PEOPLES

Given its practice of using the native peoples as the main source of labor to produce furs for the state, the Tsars had a vested interest in maintaining the highly adapted land use

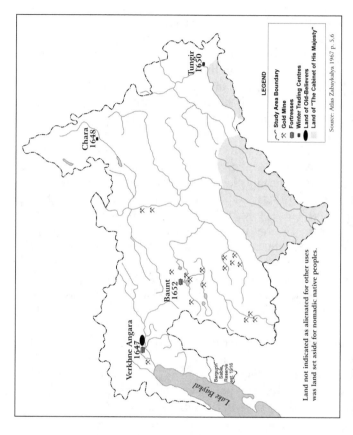

FIGURE 3.1 Historic encroachments into Evenki homelands in northern Transbaykalia.

systems of the aboriginal northerners. The Crown claimed all the land in Siberia as its own. Its very terminology regarding native peoples underscored its prejudices: all natives were identified as *inorodsty*, "aliens," literally "people of different birth." Yet, if not recognizing any inherent rights by the aboriginal northerners to their lands, Tsarist legislation eventually sought (in principle) to minimize the disruption to indigenous fur producers which settlers and even Russian fur hunters could cause.

As colonists began to arrive in significant numbers, conflicts over land use inevitably arose, both over land natives lost to colonist settlements and over extraction of natural resources from indigenous homelands. Beginning in the early 1800s, the civil court in Irkutsk, the capital of Eastern Siberia, heard several cases related to such resource conflicts. In the first decade of the nineteenth century the Governor of Irkutsk ruled that non-Russians (i.e., natives) had no exclusive rights to the land that they occupied; the government granted them only usufruct rights to the renewable resources. This judgment provided the basis for subsequent decisions which held that aboriginal peoples did not own the land and thus had no control over the extraction of its mineral wealth. Irkutsk's rulings, subsequently approved by the Tsar, only increased the potential for conflict between colonists and aboriginals (State Duma 1995).

Realizing the indeterminate nature of law over vast stretches of empire territory and the varied peoples who lived throughout this territory, in 1822 a close advisor to the Russian Tsar, Mikhail Speransky, convinced the Tsar of the need to set up a system of administration to address such resource conflicts, and to protect the native peoples in order to ensure their ability to continue to provide furs. Speransky authored a "Statute on the Administration of Aliens in Siberia." The stipulations of this statute remained in force, with minor changes, until the Bolshevik Revolution of 1917. They provided rights for "aliens" (native persons) who took up a settled way of life which were equivalent to those enjoyed by Russians. For the nomadic northerners, the statute sought to protect the economy and land base on which it depended.

To this end, the statute divided non-Russians into three categories: "settled," "nomadic," and "wandering." "Nomadic" referred to the mainly transhumant groups, who shifted camp from winter to summer pastures, while "wandering" referred to the truly nomadic peoples. Indigenous peoples of the North, including the Evenkis of Transbaykalia, fell mostly within the latter category. The state allocated to the "wandering" peoples allotments of land separate from those of other groups (the settled and transhumant non-Russians). It prohibited Russians from settling on these lands without permission. Within such allotment leasing of limited territories to Russians could occur, but only with consent of the aboriginal peoples, and under conditions set by their governing bodies. Although under the Speransky Reforms, as the statute came to be known, indigenous peoples enjoyed (at least on paper) certain exclusionary rights to the land allotments, they did not own the land. Rather, from the vantage of St. Petersburg they enjoyed rights of occupancy, usage, and administration on what had become state-owned land.

The state allotted land parcels to Native clans. Further distribution of land use rights within the clans, to obshchinas or families, was to be governed by the common law of the people to which the land had been allotted. The "Statute on the Administration of Aliens in Siberia," however, dictated the form of "indigenous" governance which would oversee such distribution. Rather than respect the existing clans of the native peoples (which in any event, as mentioned in Chapter Two, appeared to be deteriorating by the latter nineteenth century), it established its own system of "alien clans." Elders recognized by the obshchinas as the rightful Evenki leaders were often ignored, as the state identified more reliable "elders" who would be responsive to state needs. Thus, contrived clans with conscripted leaders served as an exogenously imposed organizational structure to govern the internal affairs of obshchinas, and to extract tribute and taxes. Frequently Russian officials merged Evenki clans together to form such "administrative clans" where doing so served state interests.

By the late 1800s, the state-contoured clan administration had grown to include three elected clan "elders" (with elections supervised by Russians), a Russian clerk, and a Russian appointed administrator. It was the clerk who often enjoyed the greatest power, in that he collected taxes, tribute, and the payments collected from outsiders for hunting, haying, gold-washing, or other uses of the lands allotted to the Evenki administrative clan (Orlov 1858; Shirokogoroff 1966). The "native administrations" met annually, usually in mid-winter, to deal with financial matters, including the payment of *yasak,* and the election of an Evenki judge. At these meetings Russian authorities disseminated information regarding new laws and regulations, increased tribute and taxes, and other topics.

INCURSIONS ON EVENKI HOMELANDS

While the "Statute on the Administration of Aliens in Siberia" provided legal protection of indigenous control over traditional lands, if on terms set by the state, the actual allotment of land to the "native administrations" that the statute called for was slow to occur. Where land was allotted, local officials did little to curtail the continuing encroachment on native territories by Russians. As colonization of Russia's North accelerated in the second half of the nineteenth century, indigenous obshchinas increasingly faced the threat of being pushed off their own lands.

In Transbaykalia, a non-native hunting population slowly grew, attracted by the valuable Barguzin sable. Until the second half of the nineteenth century, the number of immigrants to this remote area remained small. Then, with the discovery of gold in 1844, the pace and character of colonial ingress to Northern Transbaykalia changed. Hoping for quick riches, prospectors streamed in. Criminal and political exiles from the west joined the work force. Large Chinese and Korean populations also gathered in the vicinity of the mines and placers, comprising over ninety percent of the mining population in the years just prior to the Russian Revolution. By the end of the nineteenth century mines peppered the Barguzin Tayga (Figure 3.1). Evenkis were reduced to only twenty-two percent of the population in the western part of Northern Transbaykalia, while "Russians" (including Ukrainians, Tatars, Poles, and others) constituted sixty-six percent, and Chinese and Koreans accounted for fourteen percent (Kozulin 1991).

The nonindigenous population grew more slowly in the eastern regions of Transbaykalia, where small mines opened several decades later (Kozulin 1991). Here, though, the Tsarist government dedicated the whole southeastern section (including present-day southern Tungokochen and Tungiro–Olëkma Counties) to the "Cabinet of His Majesty" (Figure 3.1). This designation allowed the leasing of land to prospective gold guilds without any consultation with the local Native Administration.

Outright confiscation of land directly affected only small territories around the various gold lodes, whether on administrative clan lands, or lands of the "Cabinet of His Majesty." Mining and related activities, however, altered the ability of Evenkis to continue their traditional land use practices over much larger expanses. As caravans of supplies rattled along the paths toward the lodes and placers, as the noise of the gold-washing reverberated through the tayga, as herds of pasturing cattle and horses became a common component of the landscape, the wild animals, especially the moose, elk, and wild reindeer on which Evenkis depended, retreated. The miner's use of fire also changed the visage of Northern Transbaykalia. An early twentieth century account noted that "[t]races of fire can be found everywhere that the mine paths go" (Kryukov 1908, p. 63). In part ignited by carelessness, in part deliberately set, the fires purposed miners' interests. The Evenkis, or rather the Native Administrations which purportedly served the Evenkis under the Tsarist regime, had the right to levy a tax on trees cut by miners, who used the wood as fuel to thaw gold-bearing deposits. Since the tax was lower on fallen trees, miners would start fires intentionally to obtain dry wood at reduced cost. Burning also took place to clear land for agriculture. Some fires simply served aesthetic ends. Immigrants from the steppe regions of Russia, accustomed to open views, and finding the tayga scenery claustrophobic, cleared great swathes by burning. Fires destroyed hundreds of square kilometers of forest and the lichen pastures and game animals that they harbored (Shirokogoroff 1966; TsGAOR f.3977, op.1, d.372, l.6).

Indeed, in the early twentieth century, a lively debate filled the pages of the Russian journal *Hunter and Fisherman of Siberia* on the role of the Evenkis themselves in causing such fires. One contributor blamed forest fires in part on the smudge fires which herders built to protect their reindeer against biting insects, and then allegedly abandoned without properly extinguishing them (Sytin 1929). Another disputed this claim, noting the great care Evenkis took with cigarettes, smudge fires, and any other burning material (Zisser 1929). He had spent a couple of months with Evenkis of the Chara River basin, and recounted crossing a large burn, during which his companions searched for two days for food for their deer. One of his Evenki travel partners lamented, "I found but little forage…and previously this was all intact. The Russians and Koreans have crossed much territory looking for gold. They have burnt everything—now there is no forage. How will I feed my deer?" (Zisser 1929, p. 18). Fires and gold mining drove some Evenki groups to abandon their homelands in search for less disturbed areas. Many of the Evenkis now living along the Olëkma River date their arrival in this area to the latter nineteenth century; they fled from gold mining activity further south (LOZ l.1).

Construction on the Trans-Siberian Railroad in the first years of the twentieth century further stimulated the flow of immigrants into Evenki territory in Transbaykalia. Those encroaching on Evenki lands were in part uprooted peoples; nomadic Buryats forced northward as Russian agriculturists dispossessed them of their homelands and Russian hunters propelled by the expansion of agriculture. These people in turn displaced Evenki hunters and herders, pushing them farther north into the tayga, as they moved onto the Vitim Plateau and into the Olëkma tayga. Russian hunters who transgressed Evenki hunting grounds failed to observe the rights of the obshchinas to exclusive use of some of the species. They even raided Evenki *labazy*—the storehouses with small stocks of food, seasonal clothing, and equipment the Evenkis maintained to ease their loads during migrations. Russians' dogs chased down the domesticated reindeer (Tugolukov 1962). From the northeast came another pressure: Sakha (Yakuts) moving south and west. By the seventeenth century, Sakha agriculturists began settling the Chara and Muya valleys (Tugolukov 1962). When the crops they sowed froze, and when the cattle and horse husbandry they imported proved tenuous, some adopted reindeer husbandry. However, when Evenkis tried to cut hay on traditional lands close to the new Sakha settlements they faced opposition. Any kind of agriculture, it seemed, the Sakha colonists considered within their exclusive sphere of activities. They claimed the haylands to be theirs, chased Evenkis off, and confiscated cut hay (Gubelman 1925).

Along the Verkhne Angara River, between the Svetlaya and Kotera rivers, Old Believers[2] received an allotment of traditional Kindigir clan land (Figure 3.2). While the territory lost was relatively small in size, it removed from Evenki tenure a section of river and its bank which was important for fishing, for wildfowl hunting, and for trapping certain species. Losses of access to key habitat could have a deleterious impact far greater than their small areal extent would suggest.

More drastically, late Tsarist conservation concerns caused one Evenki group to suffer total dispossession of its traditional lands on the eve of the Revolution. The Shemagir clan's homelands comprised some of the most valuable hunting grounds in Transbaykalia, along the northeast shore of Lake Baykal. The position of their homeland on the lake shore made it relatively accessible, and the area was rich in Barguzin sable. Nonindigenous hunters leased the "sable rivers" which flowed into Baykal from the Shemagir Native Administration, generating quite a handsome income for the

---

2. A religious group which had split from the Russian Orthodox Church and subsequently suffered persecution; many sought refuge in Siberia.

administrative clan (e.g., 15,763 rubles in 1911). Earnings from leasing land to outsiders in fact brought Shemagir households, on the average, forty-six percent more income than that generated from other activities, including hunting (Neupokoev 1928).

However, massive overhunting of sable in the whole Lake Baykal watershed (as elsewhere throughout Siberia) resulted in falling harvests. Worried about declining populations of some of the Empire's most valuable animals, the Tsarist government resolved to establish a sanctuary for the sable's protection. It founded the Barguzin Sable Reserve in 1916 (Figure 3.1), and ousted all humans from this reserve. The Shemagir Evenkis were forced to relocate north of the reserve's border, and forbidden any hunting within the reserve. While they could rent the rivers of their new territory to outsiders, these were not as valuable. Moreover, the Shemagir themselves knew these lands less intimately, which undoubtedly made their lives more difficult in the first years or decades of relocation.

MODIFICATIONS OF EVENKI LAND TENURE

Excluding cases of wholesale dislocation, such as that experienced by the Shemagir, to what extent did paper enactments in St. Petersburg and local authorities' interference modify land tenure systems of the Transbaykal Evenkis? It appears that obshchina rights to traditional territories were not undermined but clan rights to redistribute those territories in times of need were. It may have been the exogenously-imposed clan structures, along with pressures of colonization, that eroded the autonomy and distinctness of the traditional clans, while permitting the persistence of their constituent obshchinas. In some cases the elected elders were the recognized elders of clans; in others they were not. Fissioning and fusion of traditional clans, where it served the administrative purposes of the Tsarist government, was not avoided. By the nineteenth century the consanguine clans had been fragmented, largely by state fiat (Tugolukov 1962).

The growing importance of the fur hunt itself encouraged the pre-eminence of obshchina over clan, as the socioeconomic unit producing the furs. As overhunting exhausted fur resources from watersheds, hunters had to disperse: the mobility of indigenous Siberians increased markedly. This eroded clan structure and clan territoriality. "Joint possession of the territory by all members of the community belonging to different clans became the rule" (Vasilevich and Smolyak 1964, p. 645).

The government introduced further structural changes into Evenki land tenure by allowing the Evenkis to collect taxes on lands that the government had "given" them, from Russians, Buryats, and Evenkis of other clans who used the lands for hunting, mining, haying. and so forth. This contravened an Evenki tradition of not leasing, purchasing, or selling land (Shirokogoroff 1966; V Baykitskom 1934). Land was not a marketable commodity, nor were rights to resources that it provided. In this sense, the Evenkis practiced what could be deemed Marxian concepts; labor alone added value to natural resources. Given that the clan clerks who collected such taxes were mainly Russian, the conflicts in ideologies may have been limited.

Clan administrations (or their clerks) responsible for collecting the money in any event often revealed a fairly lax attitude toward use without payment. When they did request payments, immigrants often refused. Still, taxes occasionally levied generated earnings for some groups of Evenkis, as noted above (Shirokogoroff 1966; Neupokoev 1928). At the same time, cases of interclan leases among the Evenkis themselves appeared not to be onerous, for example, an Evenki from one administrative clan paid another clan administration 50 rubles for a three-year lease (1902–1905) of a hunting territory, and harvested 2000 rubles worth of sable on this territory (Voskoboynikov 1961).

At the end of the Tsarist period, and well into the first decades of Soviet power, many Evenkis continued to enjoy tenure over their traditional obshchina territories. Modification of spatial patterns by disease, fire, encroachment, and state organization during the Tsarist period likely exceeded that of previous centuries. We must remember that, while the Evenkis recognized obshchina and clan territories, these had changed contours prior to the arrival of Russians, due to wars, famines, and other such events. We know little of this Evenki prehistory, but can surmise that incorporation into the fur trade and Russian colonization would have challenged Evenki territoriality and land tenure systems to a greater degree than had previous periods.

The state officially repudiated indigenous rights to land by its creation of "crown land." Unofficially hunters, miners, and agriculturists competed for and usurped Evenki lands. Relative remoteness from nodes of state power and population diffusion mapped a differentiated topography of encroachment across Transbaykalia; those Evenki living near gold mines and accessible sable grounds suffered complete dispossession of territories, while those farther removed from such sites hardly felt the press of state building and territorial expansion during the pre-Soviet period. The Soviet regime would prove more thoroughly hegemonic in its alteration of Evenki land tenure.

4

Evenki Land Use Reconstructed: The Soviet Era

"EQUAL BUT UNENLIGHTENED:" EARLY SOVIET POLICY TOWARD INDIGENOUS NORTHERNERS

Tsarist policy toward the northern indigenous peoples had, at least on paper, sought to protect indigenous access to land, if for its own purposes. Indigenous northerners required a paternalistic guardianship in order to ensure a flow of furs westward. In 1917, did this policy toward the indigenous northerners change, with the usurpation of power by the Soviets?

We can identify both breaks and a certain level of continuity in state relations with the Evenkis and other peoples of the Russian North between the Tsarist and Soviet periods. Both regimes claimed ownership of native homelands. Both regimes identified the peoples of the North as needing special protection, due to their "backward" nature. The Soviets, however, viewed different means of implementing protection than that used by the Tsarist government. In fact, to talk about either Tsarist or Soviet policy as a unified body is spurious; during both eras state approaches toward the native northerners shifted over time. Fundamental disagreements characterized the members of the Soviet bodies charged with northern policy formulation in the first decades of Soviet power; policy changed with the shifting balance of power between political camps. As throughout the world, ideological struggles geographically and philosophically far removed from indigenous peoples themselves came to greatly affect their lives and their homelands.

Upon assumption of power by the Bolsheviks, Soviet legislation almost immediately declared all citizens of Russia equal, and abolished the distinct status held by the "aliens." A 1917 "Declaration of the Rights of the Peoples of Russia," and the 1918 Constitution prohibited all privileges or restrictions based on racial or national background. In terms of land rights, the new government abolished all private ownership of land and natural resource on that land. Tenure was theoretically given to "those who worked the land with their own labor," while the state reserved the right to formally grant use rights to individual citizens and groups (State Duma 1995).

To oversee nationality ("ethnic") issues, the Soviets established a special ministry, *Narkomnats* (Peoples' Commissariat of Nationalities). This Commissariat was officially responsible for the northern indigenous peoples, as well as the other hundreds of peoples encapsulated within the Soviet borders. However, its attention and expertise focused elsewhere, mainly to problems along the southern frontiers of Russia. With prodding from ethnographers concerned about the fate of the northern peoples, Narkomnats recommended that a separate body be set up to deal with these peoples. Thus, in 1924, a Committee for the Assistance of the Peoples of the Northern Borderlands was established. More commonly called the "Committee of the North," this body's purpose was to protect the interests of the peoples of the North, to help guide the development of their homelands, and to establish principles for the administration of these areas (Vakhtin 1994). While poorly funded, the Committee of the North nevertheless had an impact on the development of nationality policy regarding the northern peoples during the early years of Soviet power. The Committee, in fact, consisted of two increasingly polarized factions, "conservatives" and "radicals." Land—the status of indigenous homelands—provided a major focus of their disagreement. The "conservatives" argued for the protection of indigenous peoples via secured reservations. Looking to the model of North America, they suggested that territories be set aside, under the central government's control, for the protection and development of traditional aboriginal activities. Colonists would be excluded from these areas, as would certain activities, such as the sale of alcohol and private trade. Allowed to develop toward socialism at their own pace, the northern peoples would maintain their distinctive cultures while doing so. An ideology of gradualism underpinned this approach.

The "radicals" dismissed such propositions as overly protectionist. Northern lands contained great wealth, needed for the improvement of the lives of all Soviet citizens. The natives, in helping the nonnatives extract the wealth of the North, would be more effectively drawn into socialism and modern life. To apply a model of reservations was to unnecessarily delay the natural progression of society, to unfairly hold back the indigenous northerners (Slezkine 1994).

ESTABLISHING NATIVE TERRITORIES: THE MYTH OF HOMELANDS

Out of this struggle came a compromise to designate areas over which indigenous groups would supposedly exercise effective political and administrative control. Within these territories the peoples of the North would be able to pursue a future based on traditional or nontraditional activities, according to their own decisions. In 1926, the new Bolshevik government adopted the first unified act which addressed indigenous rights to such specific territories. This act, "Provisional Regulations for the Administration of Native Peoples and Tribes of the Northern Extremes of the RSFSR," called for the establishment of native governing structures, such as clan assemblies, clan councils, county-level Native conferences, and county-level Native executive committees. These local self-government bodies were responsible, *inter alia*, for the supervision of activities within specific territories, and for the enforcement of rules regarding renewable resource harvesting (i.e., hunting and fishing).

In northwestern Transbaykalia, the local Soviets responded to this act by establishing two Evenki National Counties (Severo–Baykal and Baunt)[1] in the mid-1920s (Shubin 1967). In both counties Russians outnumbered Evenkis and dominated the county power structures. However, at lower levels of administration, in the townships[2] Evenkis were more likely to have input to some decisions. Baunt County, for instance, was subdivided into eleven townships; five of these were "national" (native) Evenki townships. The native townships existed in varying forms for approximately a decade. To what extent these offered the opportunity for self-governance is debatable; in many areas of the Russian North, where similar institutions had been set up, such councils were poorly understood and largely ignored by the bulk of the indigenous population (Vakhtin 1994). Evenki memories of the native townships in Western Transbaykalia often are positive: "Before their liquidation, in these organs of local self-administration Evenkis were the majority, which gave them the possibility of resolving problems specific to them" (Chunavlev 1988). Mostly semiliterate or illiterate, many not speaking Russian, Evenki hunters

---

1. The present-day Muya County was carved out of these in 1989. Prior to that, the borders of the two counties had been modified a number of times.

2. *Sel'skie sovety.* I use "township" here as an imprecise but commodious phrase for rural council (*sel'skiy sovet*), and later rural administration (*sel'skaya administratsiya*). Each county (*rayon*) is divided into several "townships;" a "township" might have more than one village, with one designated as the central village, in which the township's administration is located. Until 1993 such divisions were called rural councils, after this rural administration. Few people use the new term in conversation.

and herders for a few years were incorporated into the Soviet administrative apparatus, if on admittedly disadvantageous terms of power (Savin 1989).

New administrative boundaries at the county level, although ideally meant to bound areas over which relatively distinct and homogeneous groups of Native peoples would enjoy control, often hindered relations between groups closely associated by trading and cooperative labor ties. Poorly informed of indigenous social geographies, those officials charged with drawing the boundaries often sundered, rather than acknowledged the territoriality of, extant native groupings. "The zone of nomadism of the reindeer Evenkis is not limited by the boundaries of the county or even of the Buryat Republic...," noted one local Evenki (Voronin 1932, p. 191). As each county was set up, groups encapsulated within the boundaries of that county were expected to rearrange their patterns of activities to articulate with the trading posts of that county, even when neighboring ones might be closer and commonly used during certain times of the year. In Northern Transbaykalia, part of the hunting grounds of one group of Evenkis ended up within the Buryat Republic and part within the neighboring Irkutsk Province. Later shifting of county boundaries addressed this problem to some extent (Atlas Zabaykal'ya 1967).

A group of Evenkis, living in what is now the Kalar County, complained of impediments produced by the early gerrymandering: "We Tungus [Evenkis], living identical lives, are divided between four territories. Owing to the fact that we nomadize throughout the wide area, there may be hindrances on the part of various organizations.... We...need our own native county." (Zibarev 1968, pp. 260–261, quoting the Communist Party Archives of Irkutsk Province).

The Evenkis of Kalar soon received more than "their own native county." The year 1930 witnessed the establishment of Native Districts (*natsional'nye okrugi*) across the Soviet North. These districts, at the next level higher than a county in the Soviet territorial-administrative system, served as the final compromise between the "conservatives" and "radicals" in Moscow in providing indigenous peoples territorial recognition. Such a national district was established in the eastern part of Transbaykalia. The Vitim–Olëkma Evenki National District embraced what are now Tungokochen, Kalar, and Tungiro–Olëkma Counties, and for a period a section of the neighboring Amur Province. Archival records indicate that Baunt County was also considered for inclusion in this National District (Solovova 1993). Evenkis in Baunt, Tungokochen, and Kalar Counties regularly visited each other, married, exchanged reindeer for "freshening" of the herds' blood, and associated with each other in many other ways. The Vitim River, when frozen, allowed for easy intercourse. By drawing a boundary down this river, and subordinating political governance and economic organizations of the Evenkis on either side of the river to two different structures (the Buryat Autonomous Republic and the Vitim–Olëkma National District, later the Chita Province), the state hindered association of related Evenkis at several levels. Today the divide is apparent; Evenkis on each side of the river may note that they are of the same clan as those living on the other side but refer to each other as "Chitintsy" or "Buryatskiy," a difference seemingly more important than that of the common clan identity.

Did the Vitim-Olëkma District serve to empower the Evenkis as its creation allegedly intended? In 1931, at its inception, of sixty communist party members and twenty-seven party candidates, only 5 (six percent) were Evenki (Partinye 1980). At the time, Evenkis constituted roughly sixty percent of the population. While ten of seventeen townships were "native" (Evenki), minutes of district, county, and township meetings suggest that these meetings offered more opportunities to instruct the Evenkis in new Soviet ways, and to hand down dictates, than to provide for self-determination (GAChO f. R-612).

Yet many Evenki persons from Transbaykalia view the 1920s and early 1930s as a golden age in terms of the development of their rights. If the Soviet state took a paternalistic stance toward protecting native peoples, its policy recognized the importance of a degree of territorially based self-governance, at least over local issues, and of regard for specific Native customs and practices. Frequently not implemented, the letter of the law at least held out a promise of improved aboriginal rights. Evenkis and other indigenous persons consider the institutions of native administration developed during this "golden age" as worthy of rehabilitation in the 1990s (see Chapter 7).

By the mid 1930s, a major change had occurred in Soviet aboriginal policy. The radicals' power base in the Moscow Committee of the North's office increased in the early 1930s, and with it so did policies more directed to assimilation and industrial development. In 1934 the work of the Committee of the North was declared finished and the Committee disbanded. The 1936 USSR Constitution failed to mention native counties; the RSFSR's Constitution of 1937 followed suit by designating native territorial-administrative units only down to the district level. The Evenki national counties of northern Buryatia effectively turned into "ordinary" counties. Then, in 1938 the Vitim–Olëkma Evenki National District was abolished, and its territory subordinated to the newly created Chita Province.[3] In Northern Transbaykalia any state recognition of Evenki territorial rights ceased to exist.

COLLECTIVIZATION *CONTRA* COLLECTIVE ACCESS

The tragedy of the Evenkis began with the period of collectivization. At this point the *kolkhozy* became the owners of the tayga lands, later it was the *sovkhozy* and *gospromkhozy*. Forest inhabitants lost the basis of life—their clan and family lands." (Grigoreva[4] 1992)

The Soviets sought not only to restructure the political life of the indigenous northerners, but also to reshape their economic life, incorporating it into the state economy. Ac-

---

3. Most of the National Districts established in 1930 were not abolished. In 1977 they were renamed Autonomous Districts, in a move that recognized a much earlier shift in Soviet policy, from concerns regarding the native population to attention toward all those living in "land inhabited by Native peoples."
4. M. F. Grigoreva served as the president of the provincial level Association of Numerically Small Peoples of the North for the Chita Province until 1995.

cording to Marxist principles of economy, all means of production should be owned collectively. While many northern peoples had remained terribly backward in their political, economic, and social development in the eyes of Soviet theoreticians, paradoxically, class divisions had managed to emerge, especially among the reindeer herders. Soviet ideologues saw rich reindeer herders, who concentrated the indigenous means of production (the reindeer), as exploitative of their poorer clans folk. Such class divisions had to be erased, and, at the same time, the sadly backward aboriginal activities "rationalized" and modernized. Beyond these ideological motivations, a driving incentive behind the collectivization movement was the need to generate and access a surplus of foodstuffs and other goods for the growing urban populations in the Russian North.

In the western and southern areas of the Soviet Union, collectivization was rapid, forced, and brutally imposed (Conquest 1986). State officials confiscated farmers' and herders' livestock, tools and property, and turned these over to the "collective." Those who resisted were deemed "enemies of the state." Millions of Soviet citizens lost their lives during this period; yet millions of others were deported. A number of the Russian and Ukrainian inhabitants in Transbaykalia's small villages trace their parents' arrival in the area to such deportations.

Confronted with the draconian nature of collectivization as practiced in the heartland, the Committee of the North's "conservative" faction lobbied hard for a more gradualist approach tailored to the needs of the northern peoples. Communist Party resolutions initially bought into this approach, stressing the need to consider the "cultural and economic specificities" of the northern peoples. Rather than immediately establish collective farms, with all means of production and labor collectivized, the Soviets were instructed to set up "simple comradeships" among the aboriginal population, in which production (labor) of a group's main activity was collectivized, but the means of production (reindeer, traps, hunting arms, etc.) remained "private" property. Auxiliary activities would also continue to be carried out on an individual basis (Sergeev 1955). Of course, state views regarding the predominance of private property among Native northerners were ill-informed; much property was owned collectively by the obshchina.

Joining a comradeship or collective farm was to be voluntary, and open to all indigenous persons except for shamans and "kulaks." The state assigned reindeer herders to various socioeconomic categories—hired laborers, poor but independent peasants, middle peasants, and "kulaks" or exploiters—on the basis of material possessions and social relations. Kulaks were deemed "exploiters of the masses" both due to their larger reindeer herds and to their status as employers of others' labor. In a declared atheistic state, shamans, as religious leaders, were also "enemies of the people."

State officials then allocated land according to a hierarchy which favored the Soviet collective over the aboriginal obshchina, and poor over the rich. The newly formed comradeships and collective farms received the best lands; then poor individuals and formerly hired workers who had not yet joined a collective; then individuals of the "middle class." Anyone else who requested land might receive a small tract, if any remained. This meant that the richest herders, who had stewarded the best and most extensive grazing lands in the past, received usufruct rights to poor land, or none at all.

Collectivization began in western Transbaykalia by the early 1930s, and spread eastward. In its first stages, collectivization was little more than a formal moniker for the continuation of an extant indigenous system of land use. Obshchinas of one or a few families, nomadizing in their traditional territories, were now designated by names such as the "Red Hunter" or "Bolshevik" comradeship. In the early stages, the territorial boundaries of comradeships mapped closely to traditional territories (Nikul'shin 1939).

However, as the Soviets moved to consolidate comradeships into larger kolkhozy, and to exclude the "exploitative" elements of aboriginal society from these larger collectives, there were significant shifts in access to land for some Evenkis. Although membership was supposedly voluntary in the collectives, the state exerted strong pressures on the poor to join. Those who had few deer, and who mainly relied on hunting, could be pressured into joining a kolkhoz by State control over hunting arms and ammunition. Formerly these

hunting necessities had been provided by traders, sometimes on usurious terms. Now, as Soviets squeezed out and
outlawed such "capitalist exploiters" the hunter had no
means at all to obtain these goods, save "voluntary" membership in a kolkhoz. Yet, as just noted, many of the obshchinas, with few or moderate numbers of deer, were able to
continue to pursue their traditional activities on their traditional lands, agreeing simply to being designated a "comradeship" in return for rights to trade furs for guns,
ammunition, and foodstuffs at the local cooperative shop.

It was harder to force rich herders to buy into the collective system. Outright confiscation of reindeer soon became a
common tactic of the State. Some rich Evenki herders resisted by redistributing their reindeer. Since, at least theoretically, "middle peasant" and "poor peasant" households had a
choice to collectivize, and were not subject to confiscation of
their property, rich herders gave their deer to relatives and
workers, who in turn refused to collectivize and continued
to work as a group herding the deer (Tugolukov and Shubin
1969). Others simply slaughtered their deer in protest, rather than have them confiscated. Yet others ran their reindeer
into the forest and left them. As feral animals, the deer still
could be hunted.

Communist Party archives document both state repression and native response:

> In connection with the dekulakization of the house-
> hold of the kulak Protod'yakonov and the forceful
> removal of gold items and fur clothing from the dis-
> enfranchised Yegorovs in the Kalar County in 1932,
> other kulaks and the prosperous part of the native
> population, frightened by these severe measures,
> migrated to the Baunt County. The Yegorovs, fear-
> ing this pressure, threw the fate of their deer herds
> to the mercy of fate, taking a minimum (200) with
> them, and left for Nichatka. (GAChO f. R-612, op.1,
> d.88, l.63)

A few families long managed to hide such animals from
officials, and continue their herding and hunting life outside
of the Soviet system: "My grandmother...lived in the forest

up until 1964. They kept about 60 head of deer, and they maintained a nomadic way of life...They were just on their own" (Y. P., May 1994). Such families, practicing almost total self-sufficiency far removed from the Soviet-created settlements, have attained a martyr status of sorts; accounts of their survival apart from Soviet society has a folklore quality.

Reindeer, when successfully confiscated from rich herders, were to be redistributed to the poor and hired herders who owned few or no deer, or more often, were turned over to the collectives that these persons had joined. However, this "redistribution of wealth" often failed to work. Deer numbers plummeted due to the carelessness shown toward confiscated livestock. Soviet organizations would sometimes sell the deer for meat. If they did not slaughter the deer, they often assigned insufficient herders to look after the herds. By 1932 over half of the reindeer confiscated from "kulaks" and turned over to collectives in Northern Buryatia had been lost (Tugolukov and Shubin 1969). One observer noted, for instance, that "500 head of deer of the dekulakized kulak Tulbukonov (Kindigir Native Council, Severo-Baykal County) are found on the Chuya and Chaya Rivers in a completely feral state, without any supervision" (Iz Bauntovskogo 1935, p. 104). Those reindeer which were maintained by state institutions were often overexploited: "There is not a careful relation toward the deer; frequent use of deer herds for transport without discrimination are observed" (Iz Bauntovskogo 1935, p. 104). A combination of resistance on the part of Evenki herders and neglect or abuse on the part of state-founded institutions led to dramatic decreases in the number of reindeer; in the northern counties of Buryatia, reindeer numbers decreased by forty-seven percent between 1930 and 1936, and in northern Chita Province by thirty-eight percent between 1931 and 1935 (Klobukov n.d.; GAChO f.R-612, op.1, ed. khr. 196).

The large numbers of reindeer which the richer obshchinas had controlled gave them the ability, indeed the right under customary law, to control larger traditional territories. Once their deer were confiscated, even under customary law, their ability to continue to exert usufruct rights became disputable. Other Evenki herders began to colonize this pasture, by a complicated nexus of Soviet authority and customary practice. Today, struggles for obshchina lands pit those whose grandparents fled from repression against other Evenkis whose parents took their place on the herding pasture, using opportunities created by Soviet coercive measures. Yet, if the Soviets' program of dekulakization caused certain obshchina lands to become available, their cooption by members of new obshchinas follow traditional Evenki practices (Fondahl 1995; see Chapter 6).

Within the system of collectivization, farm chairpersons soon realized that the Evenkis, who had long depended on the land, needed to be able to make critical decisions about its usage. Ill informed about the land's resources, newly arrived chairpersons (brought in because of their "expertise") could only expect disastrous results if they dictated pasture rotation and hunting regimes. During the early decades of collectivized farms, such flexibility of land management was often allowed. Evenkis now turned the furs and meat of the animals which they hunted, the milk of the reindeer, and eventually the reindeer themselves, to the collective farm. Yet decisions about where to hunt and where to herd often remained with the Evenkis and continued to follow age-old patterns of respect for obshchina territories, excepting the reconfiguration of lands once belonging to the richest herders. One Evenki from the north of Buryatia, born in the early 1940s, recalled of his youth:

> Each family, say, had, well if we talk about my family, we had a stream, and its watershed, a river where my family could hunt, and then meet anew.... I was young then, but the elders of the clan met at the beginning of the hunt, at the end of the hunt, here in Bagdarin or Baunt, all the clans gathered, and say, they already determined, who was going to hunt where. (V. T., April 1994)

The description is reminiscent of those recorded by observers almost a century before (see Chapter 2). Such Evenki control over locational decisions persisted into the 1950s. Another Evenki who served in the collective farm management noted that in the 1940s and 1950s, it was "the herders themselves, they nomadized and they chose [the pastures]...they chose them themselves. Deer need moss, [it is critical] to chose a good place." (Z. N., April 1994). Evenkis knew what constituted "good places" for herding and hunting in different seasons; and knew where such "good places" were located on their traditional territories. Kolkhoz chairpersons wanting to fulfill state-imposed plans of production best used this traditional environmental knowledge.

While the collective farms introduced Russian economic activities, the traditional land-based activities of the Evenkis had to be respected and nurtured as they accounted for a large part of the farm earnings. Crop raising, although encouraged as "progressive," regularly ran into the red due to the short growing season and poor soils of Northern Transbaykalia. Cattle raising fared not much better. In the mid-1930s hunting and herding contributed sixty-eight percent of the income of Evenki comradeships in Baunt County. Another twelve percent came from handicrafts, the production of which was largely dependent on hunting and herding (Klobukov n.d.). Data from five comradeships in the Vitim–Olëkma District indicate about fifty-eight percent of their earnings stemmed from hunting and herding in 1936 (GAChO f.R-612, op.1, d.197). These figures ignored the contribution hunting and herding made toward feeding and clothing the Evenkis themselves. One economist who tried to calculate Evenki income more comprehensively, incorporating domestic usage, estimated that fur and game hunting, herding (including transport for commercial purposes), fishing and gathering accounted for ninety-three to ninety-seven percent of the income in native townships of Tungiro–Olëkma County in 1933 (Baldunikov 1936). Figures from the 1950s indicate a dependence on traditional activities that had changed little; hunting and reindeer herding (including reindeer transport) contributed seventy-six percent of northeastern Transbaykalia's kolkhoz income in 1955 (Stremilov 1970). The wiser officials, charged with reconstructing aboriginal economies, abolished the elements which they deemed most abhorrent to Soviet ideology, and tried to leave the management of what remained to be guided by aboriginal knowledge of the land and its resources.

SEDENTARIZATION AND RESETTLEMENT

The Evenki population of the [Vitim–Olëkma] District is on the whole nomadic. Traditions and practices of nomadism create strong brakes to further economic development of the District. Without the transfer of the population to a settled way of life it is impossible to develop the national wealth of the District. The nomadic way of life holds back the cultural and economic development of the District. (GAChO f.R-612, op.1, ed. khr. 197)

The above quote, from Communist Party archives of the short-lived Vitim–Olëkma Evenki District, well represents Soviet ideology on nomadism. Soviet ideology, like that of most state powers, construed nomadism as backward. Its annihilation would not only provide the means for outsiders to better utilize the "wealth" of native lands, but would also allow the reconfiguring both the economic and cultural dimensions of native society.

Only settlement, carried out on the basis of collectivization and measures of land planning, opens up the possibility of rapid economic and cultural development of the nomadic population, creates the conditions for liquidation of clan ties, and leads to a more rational use of territory. (Klobukov n.d.:31)

State policy thus sought to settle the nomads.

In Northern Transbaykalia, as elsewhere in the Russian North, collectivization proceeded hand in hand with settlement of the native population. While the first comradeships were established explicitly as nomadic collectives, their successors had assigned geographic centers. The early decades of Soviet power witnessed the creation of a network of small, predominantly Evenki villages. Distinct from the already extant Russian settlements, many of which were mining nodes, these new villages served as the central foci for the small indigenous collective farms (e.g., Ust'–Dzhilinda, Ust'–Usoy, Tungokochen, Chapo Ologo, Gulya). Others (e.g., Ust'–Tananda) grew as trading posts, where Evenki families could trade furs for groceries, ammunition, and other items. The permanent population of such villages consisted of a few Russian families involved in administration, trade, and schooling. Houses were erected for some of the Evenkis, to encourage the transition from nomadism to a sedentary life. For decades, however, these were only used seasonally. Even those persons who remained in the village due to age or infirmity would set up tents on the outskirts of the villages during the summer months. The small wooden cabins initially seemed poorly ventilated and generally uncomfortable to people who had spent their lives in the tayga (Tugolukov and Shubin 1969).

Soviet officials who sought to reshape Evenki life along the lines of Russian lifeways early realized that reindeer herders could not be settled. Instead they sought to bring their children into the settlements in order to school them, and encouraged elderly people and women to also remain in the villages. Yet many Evenkis had no interest in settling and changing their way of life. In 1931, when one group of Evenkis of Tungiro–Olëkma County were questioned about their intentions to settle, they flatly rejected the idea, even turning down offers for subsidies with which to build houses. "Learning that with the cabins also came plowing and the taxing work of a farmer instead of the free life of a hunter/trapper, the Tungus decided to resist the introduction of sedentarization." (TsGAOR f.3977, op.1, d.713, l.155). Settled life did not accord with reindeer husbandry and hunting, nor with the extensive land use that these entailed.

Poor siting of settlements proved a further deterrent to settling. Often chosen by a county executive committee, with little input from future inhabitants, the locations of the new Evenki settlements regularly favored ease of access for Russian personnel over needs of the native population. "In choosing the location for the settlement, the wishes of the Orochën were not considered", wrote one observer, in a discussion on Burul'zay in Baunt County (Gilev 1934, p. 91). Occasionally Evenki protests against such sitings prevailed; at a Native Council meeting, the Evenkis announced that they would not consider settling at Burul'zay. The village was eventually resited at nearby Ust'–Dzhilinda. Settlement, like collectivization, was supposed to occur on a voluntary principle. This frequently was not the case; "the sedentarization of the mountain Tungus was planned mechanistically, without the agreement of the Natives, without consideration of lichen pastures [for their reindeer]" (Iz Bauntovskogo 1935, p. 105). Official claims of progress in settling the Evenkis contrasted sharply with the reality of resistance to settlement; few families remained in their cabins year round, and until quite recently, many spent a significant part of the year in tents in the tayga.

Those Evenkis who "settled" in the small, dispersed villages initially experienced minor difficulties with access to their traditional territories. A small village might be visited for a few months at a time, or even serve as home for much of the year by a few members of the family, as others came and went. Small holdings of private deer (up to 20 were allowed) and access to collective farm deer allowed Evenki families to move between the villages and their traditional territories with relative ease. It was the consolidation of these settlements, and requirement of children to attend school, that began to significantly modify Evenkis' ability to use their traditional lands.

Consolidation of the indigenous settlements began almost with their very creation. Collective farms deemed too small to be economically viable, especially those near others, were soon merged. For example, a mere year after their founding in 1939, the Khulugli and Tungokochen collective farms of Tungokochen County were merged (Figure 4.1). Mergers, however, did not only affect proximate farms. In Baunt County, a collective farm member recounted discovering the merging of her farm, centered at Ugolnyy, with that of the farm at Ust'–Dzhilinda, 75 km to the south as the raven flies:

> They'd sent us off for several months to hunt for muskrat…Then we came back, and the collective farm wasn't there, it had been moved…there was nothing left where we had lived…. I came back and

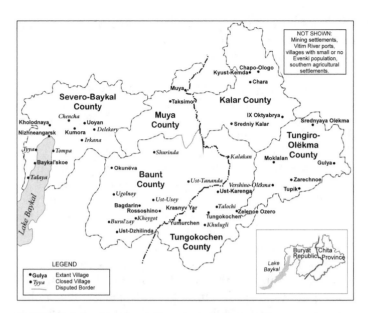

FIGURE 4.1   Northern Transbaykal Villages, Extant and Closed.

there was nothing left, no one remained. (Y. D., April 1994)

Small collective farm centers, often comprising no more than a few wooden buildings and a fluctuating number of Evenki tents, arose and then disappeared from the tayga in the course of a few years.

Settlement consolidation slowed during World War II, but then recommenced in the 1950s, the period best known for such mergings in the Russian North. Consolidation was to reduce transport expenditures (for cargo and people) to remote villages, economize on social infrastructure expenditures, and facilitate governing and administration of the population (and their economic activities). Moreover, an assumption that "modern, industrial activities" would gradually replace traditional activities underlay the consolidation policies (Pika and Prokhorov 1994).

In northern Transbaykalia, the Evenki settlement system contracted, in some places dramatically, as "nonviable" villages were identified and closed down. Collected in small hamlets in the 1930s and 1940s, Evenkis were now relocated tens or hundreds of kilometers to larger, "central" villages. In the early 1950s, in Baunt County, district officials decided to close the Evenki villages of Khoygot, Ust'–Usoy, Shurinda, and Taksimo and move all inhabitants to Rossoshino (Figure 4.1). Rossoshino, located near the county seat at Bagdarin, provided a site that was easier to supply and more amenable to the development of "Russian" activities, such as cattle raising and vegetable growing. In fact, Rossoshino, like many "viable" centers identified for consolidation throughout the Russian North, had a predominantly non-Evenki population.

Relocatees recall a decline in living standards associated with the relocation, rather than the improved one which officials promised. For instance, two members of the "Kalinin" collective farm in the "liquidated" village of Ust–Usoy recollected the lost opportunities they associated with the consolidation process:

> The "Kalinin" collective farm could have been a "millionaire" collective farm, if they hadn't closed it down, if they hadn't made us resettle at Rossoshino. There were no cattle there [in Ust'–Usoy]. Reindeer husbandry was very profitable, hunting was profitable. There were few people among whom to split the profits. It was a real Orochën collective farm. (A. B., July 1994)

> The collective farm in Rossoshino, the "1st of May," was falling apart when the merger took place. The land here is good, but boy, was it messed up!…Of course, there were more goods in the store at Rossoshino to buy, but who could buy them? We had no money. We got more money for our [work] in Ust'–Usoy—it was a richer collective farm. (M. B., July 1994)

Relocatees from Taksimo, some 400 km to the north, recounted arriving in Rossoshino to find that inadequate housing had been built; the first couple of years newly arrived families shared quarters with locals or lived in tents. Those relocated far from their traditional obshchina lands had to renegotiate access to resources on lands nearer to the central village. Pressures on lands immediately surrounding such central villages concomitantly grew. Areas farther afield remained unexploited. Harvesting of berries, nuts, and other edible and medicinal plants was carried out by more people on a smaller land base, leading to lower yields per capita and less ability to enjoy and profit from country foods and herbal remedies. While Russian-style medical services were introduced into the villages, medicines and expertise were often in short supply: local people continued to invest significant importance in the curative powers of local plants for minor ailments, in part due to the lack of options, in part due to their familiarity with such remedies. Of course, such drawbacks of population concentration had to be weighed against the advantages of increased consumer services. It has been suggested, however, that the loss of such potential subsistence activities, and the resultant social disorganization, may be one reason for the sharp rise in alcohol abuse and crime in the Native villages (I. Gemuev, April 1988; cf. Kolesnikov 1983; Pika and Prokhorov 1988).

Within a year of the massive consolidation described here, some Evenki males who had been relocated to Rossoshino were returning to their hunting grounds for the hunting season, a move required by an economy heavily dependent on fur harvests. These long sojourns back to traditional lands meant few, if any, visits with family members during hunting season, and costly transportation expenditures on the part of the kolkhoz. Relocation of Evenki families also meant that fewer women could take part in the hunt than when they had previously lived near their hunting territories. Such geographic shifts served to decrease the range of a woman's activities, her cultural and economic options and flexibility, and to channel younger women increasingly away from any level of involvement in such traditional activities. Evenki women increasingly had to accept positions as milkmaids, janitors, and other positions of low wages (and low prestige) in the villages.

Of all the Evenki activities, traditional and nontraditional, that contributed to the collective farms' economy, village consolidation least affected the geography of reindeer herders' activities. Pasture location dictated the loci of the reindeer herds. While other occupational groups increasingly clustered in the central villages of the collective farms for a major part of the year, the herders continued to live with their herds at distances up to a couple of hundred kilometers from the centers. However, more and more frequently children of school age attended school in the central villages, and elders to an increasing degree remained in the villages as well. Children, adult females, and elderly persons continued to spend summer vacation with their male reindeer herding relatives, but much of the reindeer herders' year was spent with but a few other male relatives. Their mothers, wives, sisters, and daughters were appointed jobs in the villages, or taken off to boarding school. Planners interested in the "rationalization" of reindeer husbandry deigned one woman per herding brigade sufficient to fulfill the "womanly work" needed for the herders. This "tent worker's" responsibility was to cook, sew, mend, and tend to the domestic life of the camp, such as it was. This women was usually the wife of one of the herders. Other wives, if they remained, remained "unemployed" by State-reckoning and received no wages, pensions, or other financial benefits. As these women increasingly chose (under such duress) to remain in the village, most reindeer herders enjoyed effective bachelorhood for the majority of the year, and participated little in the raising of their children.

This ruptured family life has led to several problems. Few children now master the skills required to live off the land, and especially the skills required for reindeer herding. Girls, especially, had few incentives to do so during the Soviet period, as the State offered few employment opportunities for females in reindeer husbandry, and conditions in the camps were difficult, even in comparison to the very modest comforts of Siberian village life. Evenki boys choosing reindeer husbandry as a profession chose, in conjunction, a high probability of bachelorhood. Even those who might find women who would marry them would be able to spend lit-

Yevdokiya Dogonchina and her grandson.

tle time with their partners, as the wives could not live in the camps (due to job responsibilties elsewhere) or would not (due to lack of comforts).

In fact, the gendered nature of sedentarization has been pinpointed as one of the key causes of the demise of reindeer husbandry in Northern Transbaykalia:

> Previously, women herded the deer. Now it's the men. Women tended the calves, tied them up. The cows came, they milked them, then let the calves loose. Men don't do this, and this has led to a decrease in the herds. (M. M., July 1994)

Planners interested in "rationalizing" herding failed to recognize the specificities of Transbaykal reindeer herding, in which women played a far more active and important role than was common elsewhere in Siberia. Today, women herders currently are few and far between, although those who remain are acknowledged to be among the best workers left in the field. Female herders' special knowledge of the deer and of the land on which the deer thrived was ignored by the state; this indeed may be one key explanation in a decline in reindeer numbers by over fifty percent during the Soviet period.

SOCIALIST LAND ENCLOSURE

In the 1970s, Northern Transbaykalia's collective farms (*kolkhozy*) were reorganized into state farms, *sovkhozy*. This entailed further consolidation: fifteen herding-hunting kolkhozy were merged into eight *sovkhozy* (state farms) and two *gospromkhozy* (state hunting enterprises).

Economically the restructuring from kolkhoz to sovkhoz was supposed to rationalize expenditures among both the traditional and nontraditional farm activities, and to increase the profit margin of these activities. Sovkhozy, in which both the means and relations of production belonged to the state, were considered a higher rung on the socialist ladder of economic organization. As the size of the farms grew, the chance of an Evenki or even a local person serving as chairperson diminished. Management became dominated by "newcomers:" Russians, Ukrainians, and others from outside of the region, who were trained in management skills or agronomy. Few had experience in the traditional fields.

Studies of the carrying capacity of pastures and hunting grounds, carried out in the 1970s, gave the sovkhozy a supposed basis for "rationalizing" traditional activities. One of the most damaging measures to *de facto* Evenki control of land was that of dividing the holdings of state farms and hunting enterprises into separate lots, each big enough for one or two state hunters, and allocating these to individuals. Under the kolkhoz system, Evenki obshchinas could still function as such to a degree on the farm lands. The new structure made this harder: hunting grounds were divided into parcels, the size of which accorded to "scientific" studies of potential harvest yields for fur bearers (Figure 4.2). The sovkhoz chairperson then allotted these to (almost exclusively male) hunters. Each hunter was responsible for activities on that land. Only as many positions as state hunters existed as parcels, thus leading to a number of Evenkis being squeezed out of this profession. Even where new parcel boundaries partially followed old obshchina territories, some family members might lose the right to hunt on their age old lands, as new norms now stated that the lands could only support a limited number of hunters.

This socialist land enclosure then was taken a further step. During the 1980s, hunting parcels increasingly were re-

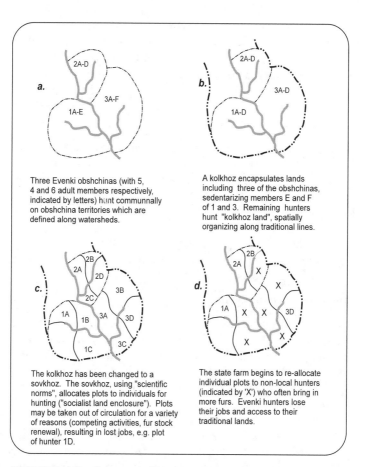

a. Three Evenki obshchinas (with 5, 4 and 6 adult members respectively, indicated by letters) hunt communnally on obshchina territories which are defined along watersheds.

b. A kolkhoz encapsulates lands including three of the obshchinas, sedentarizing members E and F of 1 and 3. Remaining hunters hunt "kolkhoz land", spatially organizing along traditional lines.

c. The kolkhoz has been changed to a sovkhoz. The sovkhoz, using "scientific norms", allocates plots to individuals for hunting ("socialist land enclosure"). Plots may be taken out of circulation for a variety of reasons (competing activities, fur stock renewal), resulting in lost jobs, e.g. plot of hunter 1D.

d. The state farm begins to re-allocate individual plots to non-local hunters (indicated by 'X') who often bring in more furs. Evenki hunters lose their jobs and access to their traditional lands.

FIGURE 4.2 Schematic Representation of Land Tenure Changes Among the Evenkis of Transbaykalia.

assigned from Evenki to non-Evenki hunters. Evenki hunters often produced fewer pelts per parcel than did their
Russian counterparts. Farm chairpersons have attributed
this to "deformations of character" (i.e., laziness and drunk-
enness) among the Evenki. Evenkis themselves explain the
differential harvests otherwise:

> If an Evenki has a territory, if he has received an al-
> lotment, he knows that there are five or six deer or
> moose, that he can cull one for meat for himself, but
> that he shouldn't take any more. He already knows
> this. He knows how many musk-deer are there. But
> an immigrant hunter comes, and female [deer] or
> not, he culls everything, he collects his money, and
> it's out of there for him. But we approach things a
> bit differently: if you cull everything today, tomor-
> row you'll be hungry." (A. T., April 1994)

Non-local hunters don't "know" the land, and don't have a
vested interest in coming to "know" it; their ignorance
ensures in the short term better rates of harvest, and in the
long-term, depletion of the fauna that serves as the basis of
the traditional Evenki activity of hunting (cf. Anderson
1991, 1992).

Another critical step toward disruption of Evenki culture came from the specialization inherent in the state farm
system. The gospromkhozy were set up to concentrate specifically on hunting, and had little incentive to encourage reindeer herding, other than as an auxiliary activity which
supported hunting (as a means of transport). Herding was
left to the sovkhozy, which were also involved in cattle raising and vegetable growing. As described in Chapter 2, during the pre-Soviet period reindeer herding and hunting had
complemented each other. Few Evenkis pursued only one
or the other. The combination of these two main activities
lent a flexibility to one's livelihood that helped ensure making it through bad epizootics (i.e., animal epidemics) and
poor fur-harvest years. While during the 1950s reindeer
herding had produced substantial income separate from
hunting, such as transporting geological reconnaissance and
surveying parties and their equipment, by the late 1960s this

income had dried up. Meat production from reindeer herds was still limited. Much of the contribution of reindeer husbandry was "invisible" as it had been in the pre-Soviet and early Soviet period—reindeer still provided an inexpensive means of transport during hunting, but did not generate much income on its own. As sovkhozy (the state farms) lost part of their share of hunting to gospromkhozy (the more specialized state hunting enterprises), reindeer husbandry appeared as a red-line item, irrational to support with resources. Increasingly gospromkhozy hired Russians, who used other means of transport to hunt. The crucial link between herding and hunting increasingly severed, both sovkhozy and gospromkhozy tended to ignore reindeer husbandry and failed to invest in its development.

INDUSTRIAL DEVELOPMENT AND ENVIRONMENTAL DEGRADATION

Concomitant with the aforementioned changes in the economic and social structure of Evenki life, was the degradation of their homelands by industrial development. In comparison with the oil bearing homelands of the Khanty, Mansi, Nentsy, and Sel'kup peoples of Western Siberia (see Appendix 1), or with the mineral-rich homelands of the Saamis of the Kola Peninsula and the Evenkis and Dolgans of the southern Taymyr Peninsula, the Evenkis of Northern Transbaykalia have suffered less devastation of their homelands. Until the 1970s industrial development remained fairly circumscribed. Yet increasingly, Evenki access to land and the ability to continue pursuing traditional activities has been compromised by environmental damage to critical habitat.

As early as the 1930s, Evenkis complained about Russians overharvesting fur species. At a meeting of the Kalar Clan Council in 1931, for instance, Evenki representatives discussed the need to establish a hunting reserve (zakaznik), in which the hunting of certain species would be proscribed. Prohibiting all hunting was even suggested, but opposed as unrealistic. An earlier meeting had acknowledged the need for continued year round subsistence hunting rights for the Evenkis, even if other restraints were put in place. At an assembly of the Tungiro–Olëkma County Executive Political Committee in the same year, Evenkis complained about losing their best hunting grounds along the Tungir River to Russian colonists (GAChO f. R-612, op.1, ed. khr.10, 12; f. R-927, op.1, d.2).

Such protests against the increased penetration of Russians into Evenki homelands continued, if with little effect. Given the repressive nature of the Soviet state, we find no mention of resistance in the contemporary literature. Such resistance is becoming known only now. One geologist reminisced of an incident he witnessed in the 1950s, in which several Evenkis blockaded building equipment's access to a tayga tract when they discovered plans to build a geologist town on prime grazing grounds in the Severo–Baykal County (V. V., April 1994). The blockade failed, the village of Pereval was erected, and after a decade of reconnaissance, was abandoned. Other similar incidents undoubtedly occurred, small in scale but extraordinarily courageous given the potential severity of repression. These local histories of defense of homeland have yet to be documented.

The year 1958 witnessed the delineation of a military test range on the homelands of the Evenkis in the Tungokochen County (Aruneev 1992). For several herding families—the Garpaneevs, Dushinovs, Kopylovs, Dmitrovs, Zaguneevs, and Kirillovs—the rich pasture lands on which they had depended were decimated. "Now this land is a desert. It burns each year from falling rockets" (Aruneev 1992). Rockets occasionally fell outside of the test range as well. Villagers in Tungokochen perceive that the testing has not only damaged traditional activities but has created health threats; the Karenga River, from which the village draws its drinking water, flows from the test range. Elevated rates of cancer and intestinal disorders are popularly inferred to stem from the pollution of the Karenga River.

Fires have reshaped the ecology of the tayga in Northern Transbaykalia and have compromised the ability of Evenki herders and hunters to pursue their traditional land-based activities. The tayga has always burnt from natural lightening strikes. But burning has much accelerated due to anthropogenic fires. Military testing contributed; geologists, reconnaissance parties, and careless hunters have also caused an increase in burning. Destruction of winter pasture by fires in cases required the culling of reindeer in order not to overtax the remaining forage base (Zuev 1984; *Sovetskiy Sever* 31 March 1983; Aruneev 1989).

By the late 1970s the Evenkis began to voice concerns about the damage associated with the building of the Baykal-Amur Mainline Railroad (BAM) through their homeland (Figure 1.1). The BAM contributed to environmental degradation of Evenki homelands in a number of ways. "In building the "railroad of the century," the [central] powers dispossessed reindeer herders, hunters, fishers, and the whole local population. In dissecting the region by a 330 km zone of railroad, which took out reindeer pasture and hunting ground, in spoiling the water of the major river of the region, the Chara," the BAM compromised the physical and cultural well-being of the Evenkis (Snegur 1993, quoting a letter by the Association of Numerically Small Peoples of the Chita Province). The swath cleared for the rail line, parallel service road, and electric lines was not great in width, but it severed domestic reindeer and wild ungulate migration routes. The BAM caused both serious pollution of the Chara, and recurrent flooding of one Evenki village (Chapo Ologo). Most significantly, the building of the BAM brought in a large contingent of laborers—"Bamovsty" ("BAM-ers"). This migrant labor force made itself infamous among the local population by its disregard for nature and of the local way of life. During off-hours, the Bamovtsy enjoyed game and fur hunting and fishing, in direct competition with the local population. They poached domesticated reindeer. Accusations abounded of Bamovtsy using alcohol to steal sable and other pelts from the Evenkis. They allegedly practiced little care with fires. Perhaps only a small percentage of BAM laborers participated in such behavior, but this select group earned a reputation for the lot. As one Evenki complained,

All around the forest was burnt or cut, and where are we supposed to hunt? So the plan [set by the state for fur harvests] goes unfulfilled. The Bamovsty don't know evil. Their all-terrain vehicles, cars, motorcycles, even helicopters reach into our whole territory. Is it time to give the Bamovsty a fur plan to fulfill? (Snegur 1989, quoting a message sent by the Association of Numerically Small Peoples of the Chita Province to the Supreme Soviet of the USSR).

The BAM's course in part was determined by the topography, in part by the location of mineral resources: asbestos, molybdenum, and others. Of the greatest importance in Northern Transbaykalia is a world-class copper site at Udokan, south of Chara in Kalar County. While depressed copper prices and serious potential challenges regarding air pollution have slowed the project, recent foreign investment interests suggest that this project may go ahead (Bond 1996). The Evenkis of Kalar County have been especially concerned about the development of Udokan:

Our ethnic land will surely become disfigured, a place for us here has not been considered, and no one suggests what will be substituted for it, our losses concern no one. (Snegur 1993)

Gold mining has been another major source of concern, especially in Baunt, Tungokochen, and Tungiro–Olëkma Counties. Gold-bearing sites are scattered throughout Northern Transbaykalia, especially in the three more southerly counties. Much is placer gold and is mined with dredges. Mechanical disruption of river beds increases silt loads, and chemicals used to extract the gold from the surrounding material (arsenic, cyanide) pollute the waters.

See, if you had come in the summer, the water would be yellow. There's nothing to drink, nowhere to wash. Nowhere to swim, nothing. Formerly, the water was so very clean, you could see the stones. And now, what turbidity!...And there are no fish, we have nothing. (G. A., May 1994)

The Evenkis of Northern Transbaykalia, like indigenous groups throughout the world, are not opposed to development. They are opposed to "development" which undermines their ability to pursue activities which are culturally as well as economically important to them, and they are opposed to "development" on their homelands, directed by outsiders, from which they enjoy no benefits. The Soviet period allowed for essentially no opportunity to the Evenkis to negotiate industrial development programs for greater benefit and less degradation. Today's new environment holds some promise; in a climate of uncertain land ownership, Evenkis in Tungiro–Olëkma County initiated negotiations with one gold mining guild, promising to moderate their claims to land in return for the guild providing improved services to a remote Evenki town near the mining site. They have also adamantly pushed the county administration to require all gold mining operations to meet federal pollution standards, which on paper are quite strict.

The concern with gold and other mining, infrastructure construction, and any industrial development is that in the past it has inflicted too much damage on Evenki homelands, and provided too little in return:

> If they behaved well toward us...if they treated us as the owners of our county, if they paid us in kind deeds, we would fight with them. We know the state needs gold. We know this very well, that this determines the riches of the country. But we are people after all, and we want to live! (Ye. M., May 1994)

For the Evenkis, the Soviet period brought a parceling of traditional lands, sometimes along recognized boundaries, sometimes not. It transferred the "ownership" of land "to the people" in theory; in practice land became controlled by economic ministries—of forestry, mining, defense, and so forth. Land available for Evenki use shrunk considerably, partly due to competition from other users, partly due to removal of Evenkis from their territories via the processes of sedentarization and the forced relocation that was a part of a larger program of farm consolidation. Moreover, much of that land which remained under partial Evenki control suffered a radical social restructuring. No longer was it obshchinas that worked the land communally; rather, the state invested responsibility in individual state hunters. It is on this backdrop that the Evenkis now negotiate for land rights.

5

Collapse of Union, Ascent of Indigenous Rights

PERESTROYKA AND INDIGENOUS AGENDAS FOR REFORM

Threats faced by the Evenkis to their cultural and physical well-being hardly could be addressed during much of the Soviet regime. To complain about the system, to protest state policies invited retribution in the form of job loss, official harassment, a term in jail—and during the most severe periods of repression—even death. Evenkis had early experienced such repression. Today individuals will quietly list the names of repressed relatives, friends, and acquaintances (not all had "protested" the system): Ivan Aruneev, Yakov Bylynov, Prokopiy Kirillov, Mikhail Kopylov, Yekaterina Kopylova, Sergei Molchanov, Chikoy Potchëtkin, Zakharov.... In the 1930s and 1940s "the majority of literate Evenkis were repressed. Some returned to their native tayga, others disappeared for ever, to the snowy Kolyma" (Lorgoktoev 1992). Those repressed included shamans and political leaders (literate and otherwise), the latter often hand-picked by the Soviets. Their crime may have been no more than offering a critical comment on the way their lives were being manipulated, sometimes not even this.

Mikhail Gorbachev's policy of *glasnost* (openness), launched in the mid-1980s, admitted criticism as a healthy, rather than harmful, attribute to the development of Soviet society. At last concerned academics and indigenous peoples themselves could depict a more realistic representation of the situation of Native northerners, little known outside of the North. A silence-shattering article, published in 1988 in the main journal of the Communist Party, painted a frightening picture of native populations facing extremely low life expectancies, living in horrendous conditions, losing language and culture, and seemingly threatened, in some cases, with extinction (Pika and Prokhorov 1988).

"The Big Problems of the Small Peoples," as the article was titled, set off an avalanche of responses. Articles by native leaders appeared in many of the major Soviet daily newspapers and literary weeklies (e.g., Aypin 1989; Nemtushkin 1988a, 1988b; Rytkheu 1988; Sangi 1988). These editorials decried the treatment of their homelands as resource depots and themselves as "younger siblings," and called for an end to "paternalistic protection" on the part of the state and the rape of their lands by the various ministries.

By 1989, a group of Native leaders had formed a federal-level Association of Numerically Small Peoples of the North. The Association held its first congress in March 1990. Speeches recounted loss of lands, environmental destruction, forced relocation, linguistic and cultural assimilation, and the social malaise which characterized too many native settlements. The Congress drew up a platform which demanded a renegotiation of aboriginal-state relations, including those policies guiding land rights and self-governance over those lands (Materialy 1990).

The federal level association was quickly reproduced at the lower levels—republican, provincial (*oblast'*), district (*okrug*), county (*rayon*), and village—partly in the hope of channeling information on indigenous needs and demands up the hierarchy, and diffusing information downward on opportunities for funding and other support that the Russian government began to create. In Transbaykalia, the Evenkis of Buryatia and Chita each organized such a system of representation. Within this newly constituted aboriginal rights movement, Evenki women accepted a significant burden of the leadership. In the past, while Evenki women lived in a patriarchal and patrilocal system of social organization, and men held the highest positions of influence, they had enjoyed a voice in decision making at the clan and obshchina level. Older women especially became authorities among the people (as did older men). This role had been undermined to some degree during the Tsarist period by Russian identification of males as the obvious members of Evenki society with whom to confer on trade and political matters. During early Soviet years, some attempt was made to reelevate the position of women in the political system; today the outcome of female leadership is in part a legacy of differential experiences of assimilation, as discussed in Chapter 6.

Over the next few years the federal Association's platform and leadership both went through a refinement process. Concerns with the urban-based leaders being "out of touch" with the typical villager's needs (seventy-four percent of indigenous Siberians are rural residents) has led to a number of changes in leadership. If the leaders in Moscow were concerned with increasing power and representation of native peoples, the villager wanted adequate housing, a secure source of income, a clean water supply, and the ability for her or his children to have a genuine choice in whether to pursue a traditional or nontraditional occupation. However, internal controversies between village priorities and those of the Moscow-based leaders little hindered a strong external lobby, which worked, with the help of nonindigenous support organizations, to hector the federal government and president to pass a series of legislative acts which began to promote indigenous rights. A Deputies' Assembly of Numerically Small Peoples of the North, Siberia, and the Far East was established in 1991; and Yevdokiya Gaer, a Nanay woman, organized an International League for the Survival and Development of Minority Peoples (1992). Action has not been limited to the federal level: as the Russian Federation political system devolves power to its constituent republics and provinces, republican constitutions have also confirmed aboriginal rights.

RUSSIAN LAND REFORM AND ABORIGINAL RIGHTS

Renegotiation of state-aboriginal relations, including rights to land, has occurred against a backdrop of broader legislative reform. Pivotal to the collapse of communism and move toward a market economy has been the privatization of land. Reformers in Russia see this as necessary for several reasons, not the least of which is reviving an ethic of responsible land use by restoring land ownership to land users. Decentralization of management is supposed to improve agricultural returns and decrease environmental degradation. In 1990 a law on private property formally ended the state's monopoly on the ownership of land. The year 1991 saw the introduction of a Land Codex, and in 1993 President Yeltsin legalized the purchase and sale of land. Coupled with these legislative initiatives are a set of acts on the reorganization and dismantling of the kolkhoz and sovkhoz system, and the transfer of their lands to their workers for private use.

With the transfer of land from state to private ownership beginning, what rights do aboriginal peoples have over their age old homelands? Private ownership seems anathema to indigenous cultures and the land requisites of traditional activities. Communal land possession characterized aboriginal tenure, as was noted in Chapter 2. How can the more ubiquitous trends of privatization mesh with the needs of indigenous peoples for land tenure systems which support ways of life critical to their cultural persistence?

This dilemma has been confronted, but not yet successfully addressed. Legislatively, indigenous access to land, resource, and cultural autonomy has improved somewhat, via a number of federal decrees, presidential edicts, and federal laws, both those specifically dealing with indigenous rights and those containing articles or clauses which acknowledge such rights. Importantly, the 1993 Russian Federation Constitution entrenched wider rights to numerically small indigenous peoples "in accordance with generally recognized principles and normal of international law and international treaties of the Russian Federation" (Konstitutsiya 1993, p. 26). If upheld, this would require conformity with recent international conventions such as the International Labor Organization Convention 169 ("On Indigenous Peoples and Peoples Leading a Tribal Way of Life in Independent Countries").

Not only has the Russian Constitution addressed indigenous rights, but articles on indigenous usage of land and resources are also found in several of the seminal laws which guide the reconfiguration of post-Soviet society in Russia. For instance, the newly revamped Law on Environmental Protection (1991), Law on Subsurface Resource (1992), and Bases for Forest Legislation (1993), all contain clauses offering recognition of the need for distinct relations between the state and aboriginal peoples (Kryazhkov 1994).

In fact the sheer proliferation of legislation, and rapidity with which it has been churned out, has resulted in not only confusion, but also internal contradictions in Russia's legal code. "Here everything is without order, every day there is another law," complained the head of the Land Reform Committee in Tungiro–Olëkma County (V. N., May 1994). Confronted with conflicting legislation, republican and provincial governments often interpret and implement it to their advantage. Sometimes they simply ignore it, allegedly waiting for the federal government to rationalized its profusion of legal acts. Evenkis and other indigenous persons, divided by political boundaries and under governments of varied persuasions regarding the tempo and dimensions of reform, experience spatial incongruities in their ability to enjoy these reforms (see Chapter 6).

Most critically, the legislation passed to date falls short of guaranteeing Evenki rights to ownership of land. It stipulates allotting land to indigenous groups, setting aside protected areas for their traditional activities, and giving substantial self-governance powers to local governments, which can be predominantly native. Yet the federal government, or its subjects (republics, provinces, and districts) remain the "owners" of aboriginal lands. A "Law on the Legal Status of Numerically Small Peoples of the North," which addresses such issues, has been circulated in draft form since the early 1990s, but as of early 1997 had not been passed; prospects for adoption seem ever dimmer (Murashko 1996).

LAND CLAIMS IN SIBERIA: VARIOUS APPROACHES

We have just identified three distinct but interleaved approaches to improving indigenous control over land resources. The first, land allotments to indigenous obshchinas, summons pre-Revolutionary forms of indigenous land tenure by endorsing the obshchina as the appropriate locus of control over land and its renewable resources. An obshchina is defined as "a voluntary unification of families and properties from among [indigenous] rural inhabitants for collaborative development in the management of deer pastures and hunting and fishing grounds" (Draft Law n.d., §6). At the basis of this legislation we find an aim of reinstating communal control over land and resource use which characterized most northern indigenous peoples' traditional land tenure systems (Chapter 6).

The second approach looks to the early Soviet decades, when the state initially gave territorial recognition to indigenous peoples through the creation of national counties and districts. It allows for the (re)creation of national counties, and of native villages as well. Hand in hand with a new law on local self-government, which devolves greater power to village and county level administrations, this approach allegedly intends to create the possibility of *native* self-government at the local level (Chapter 7).

The third approach we might characterize as looking toward the future in demarcating substantial tracts of land for traditional activities, land which is not alienable for other uses without the agreement of indigenous peoples themselves (Chapter 7). If less than fifty percent of indigenous northerners are directly involved in reindeer herding, hunting, fishing, and gathering as a main occupation, these activities still defined the core of indigenous identity. A major threat to the traditional activities, and one which the creation of an archipelago of relatively small obshchina lands insufficiently addresses, is an eroding land base for such activities in the Russian North. Indigenous leaders have called for the establishment of "territories of life" (Aypin 1989), zones of significant size from which nontraditional activities would be barred. More recently scholars have noted that, with a rocky transition toward a market economy which to date has entailed the collapse of northern services and industry, the traditional activities will play an ever-increasing role in daily survival (Pika and Prokhorov 1994). Thus, protecting their land base is of critical importance. Even some persons less committed to indigenous rights see this approach as one worthy of support in its ability to effect environmental protection of critical and threatened habitat.

In advancing legislative initiatives that call for such measures as the allocation of land to obshchinas, the creation of native territorial-administrative units, and the establishment of protected territories, the Russian Federation's government has conceded that control over land and resources underlies peoples' ability to survive. It also has recognized that a failure to negotiate indigenous rights to land and resources will perpetuate uncertainty regarding the futures of northern lands and resources. Such uncertainty will continue to obstruct economic development of the Russian North, affecting all Russian citizens. We have witnessed analogs for this in other parts of the Circumpolar North. Two examples suffice: uncertainty regarding the legal status of indigenous homelands stymied economic development in the pre-Alaska Native Claims Settlement Act situation with hydrocarbon and other resources in Alaska (cf. Osherenko 1995). And, as treaty negotiations commence in British Columbia, resource development remains hindered by uncertainty, especially in the forest industry. In the Russian North neither comprehensive legislative empowerment nor the implementation of the existing legislation have been realized. The next chapters discuss the Evenkis' experience with harnessing the power of these legislative reforms in Northern Transbaykalia.

6

Obshchina Lands: Progress and Pitfalls

OBTAINING OBSHCHINA LANDS: PROCEDURES IN NORTHERN TRANSBAYKALIA

To begin to examine "land claims" in Northern Transbay-kalia, we might follow the footsteps of one imaginary individual in petitioning for an allotment. "Stepan"[1] has decided with his wife and his younger brother to form an Evenki obshchina; Stepan's adult son will also be considered a member. Stepan lives in a village removed from the county center by a half-day's drive overland. The state farm where he worked as a hunter has collapsed; he no longer receives wages, hunting ammunition, weapons, or any other support from it. He has received a rifle from the local Evenki Association, and plans to pursue hunting. With little experience in reindeer herding, the members of Stepan's

---

1. Like Basuk of Chapter 2, "Stepan" is an composite portrait of different individuals' experiences in petitioning for a land allotment, recounted to me during fieldwork, 1992–1994, and of a personal experience in travel to one of the outlying villages. There is nothing extraordinary in this fictitious account; real histories, as recounted here, often contain much greater hardships than those offered here.

obshchina at present intend to forego plans to develop that industry. They envy their neighbors who can pursue it, as it provides a cheap alternative to snowmobile and other fuel-driven transport. But their education included almost no relevant training in how to manage reindeer. Stepan's parents herded: many years ago his brief summer vacations were spent at his father's camp. His mother moved to town when he entered school, although he was not allowed to live with her, residing instead at the boarding school dorm.

Stepan's lack of recent income means that he can't afford the weekly plane that flies from his village to the county center. Plane ticket prices indeed have inflated several times faster than wages. Is he any better off than a cousin who lives in a village to which planes have stopped flying altogether? He can't really see the difference—few villagers' salaries allow the trip by air, even when paid. Perhaps his main advantage stems from the fact that his village lies only six hours from a maintained gravel road, whereas his cousin must travel fourteen hours overland. He remembers when a few years ago airfares allowed both him and his cousin to head south with their families a couple of times a year.

To submit a petition for an obshchina, Stepan does need to visit the county center. He learns through the village grapevine that an acquaintance is heading to the center in a few days, in a "Truman," an old but sturdy army-issue pickup truck. The man has already promised rides to several others; Stepan will have to ride in the back. Travel will be touch-and-go, for it is April and the frozen tract that connects his village to the nearest gravel road will soon thaw. That is why he must travel now: in a few week's time his ability to reach the center by ground transport will evaporate, and he will have to wait until next November when the grounds again freeze hard enough to support vehicular travel.

Stepan tries to call the center several times to ascertain whether the officials he needs to confer with will be there. In Stepan's village you can count the phones on two hands: the telephone office boasts two, which serve the public, and a few other governmental offices also have them. Much of the next few days the connection between his village and the county center is down. Once he reaches the County Committee on Land Reform's secretary, he can hardly hear her. He shouts the chairperson's name into the phone several time. She screams back, "What? What? Speak louder! I can't hear you!" Finally, "He's not here," and then a click. She has slammed down the receiver before he can ask when the chairperson will be back. Stepan heaves a resigned sigh and returns home.

A small group gathers two evenings later, on a gray night promising the imminent arrival of snow. Stepan and his fellow travelers line the back of the pick-up with reindeer hides and a bearskin to make the journey more comfortable. They stretch canvases over the back to provide shelter from the snow. They can't begrudge the cold weather; it is what permits travel this late in the season.

Two hours out, the group stops at the highest pass between their village and the next. The truck's passengers—nine in all—empty out of the cabin and back. They open a bottle of vodka and packages of sausage, bread, apples, and candy. One of Stepan's co-travelers takes a bit of each of these to a carved figure aside the road, offering each in turn with a quiet supplication. The rest of the group more casually toss offerings to the local spirits, in order to assure a safe journey. They pass the bottle and foods around (the driver assiduously avoids the former), and climb back into the "Truman." This ritual will be repeated twice more at other summits by all of the truck's inhabitants, Evenki and Russian alike.

Stepan dozes off. A sharp thud wakes him. It is snowing hard. The driver, trying to maneuver through poorly visible drifts, has driven off the tract. The truck empties out. Stepan's female co-travelers in the back join the two women in the truck's cabin; the men set to extracting the truck from mud and snow. In two hours time they have managed to free the truck. Hands freezing, body aching, Stepan accepts another shot from the vodka bottle, although he rarely drinks. Two of his co-travelers are already well inebriated, and soon pass out in the back of the truck.

As the dawn arrives, the truck cranks up the last hill of snow-covered dirt onto the gravel road. From here travel will be smoother, although the county center still lies another six hours away. The travelers stop in the small village that lies at the end of the paved road. Since the cafeteria closed down last year, they awaken a distant relative of one of the travelers to ask for a bit of hot tea. Sleepily, the relative agrees. Refreshed, and promising to deliver some medicine she needs from the center on the way back, they return to the truck.

They pull into the county center in mid-afternoon. Stepan first goes to a relative of his wife to spruce up, then walks over to the governmental office. The county center is not much more impressive than his home village, rows of dilapidated wooden houses built in the 1930s and 1950s. A muddy school yard. A small, scrappy bakery, exuding delicious aromas of fresh bread. As in his own village, children arriving on foot and by bike to buy the fresh loaves. Plenty of stray dogs hovering outside, eternally hopeful. The county center does contain more modern-looking government offices and a several-bed hospital. Stepan always feels shy talking to the officials here, though; they seem somewhat more alien than the landscape of the center itself. Their Russian is more cultured, their clothing more refined, their manners more affected. They all are Russians or Buryats. Not an Evenki anywhere in the offices. He laughs a bit to himself—they wouldn't last long in the forest. Or, perhaps, even in his village. Theirs is a different world, and they often serve as officials in the county center for only a few years, soon moving on to more central locations in the province.

Stepan finds that he will indeed have to wait two days before the chairperson of the Land Reform Committee, with whom he needs to confer, returns from the capital. He will miss his ride back home. His wife's relative helps him find another. He spends the time visiting other relatives and acquaintances, repairing a related widow's home and watching TV, a pleasure since electricity in his own village has been sporadic in the last few months.

Finally, Stepan's meeting takes place. The chairperson announces that the lands which he wants for his obshchina—the lands on which he and his brother have hunted for two decades—have already been petitioned for. Yes, it is probably a misunderstanding, but there is little the chairperson can do at this point. He is lucky that the petition of the other obshchina is still pending approval; there is time to intervene. The chairperson has just learned, during his visit to the capital, that the provincial government is working on some rules that will govern the resolution of such cases. Stepan has two choices: to await such rules, or to go on to the capital to present his case.

Stepan is almost out of cash. He needs to consult with his wife and brother. He dreads a trip to the provincial capital; he knows no one there, and hotels and food are ghastly expensive; officials seem for the most part condescending and hard to talk to; and how he will get there is a puzzle. He returns home in the back of the next truck headed to his village, over the melting tract, in what is obviously the last trip of the year, pondering what to do. Life, if not as interesting, was certainly easier and more assured during Soviet rule.

◊   ◊   ◊

Federal legislation charged the republican and provincial governments with allocating obshchina lands (O neotlozhnykh 1992). In Transbaykalia the Buryat Republican and Chita Province governments devolved the job of land allocation to county governments, with a requirement to consult with local Evenki associations. At all levels, officials' interest in land reform, and specifically in indigenous land rights, varies. Personalities of individuals involved in the process—Evenki leaders, Evenki petitioners, land reform committee officials, heads of county administrations and republican/provincial officials—each contribute to the process of obshchina land allotment.

The process of petitioning for an obshchina allotment of land involves several steps, as intimated in the foregoing account of Stepan. A group of Evenkis interested in pursuing traditional activities declares itself an obshchina and draws up a charter for what they intend to do—hunt, herd reindeer, fish, hay, and so forth. An obshchina may include non-Evenki members, but at least fifty percent of the members should be Evenki (G. S. Balkhanov, chairperson of the Baunt County Land Reform Committee, 18 April 1994). Some officials suggest seventy percent as a minimum. An obshchina's menu of activities may include nontraditional ones, but these should be auxiliary to traditional pursuits, according to federal legislation. The charter, a budget for activities, and a request for a land allotment to support the activities is forwarded to the county's Committee on Land Reform. This committee reviews the petition for conflicts with other users, consults with other county committees (e.g., on environmental protection) via an interdepartmental commission incorporating interested parties, and makes a recommendation to the county government to allocate the land or refuse the petition. When the petition involves land for hunting (as it almost always does) counties within Buryatia send their positive recommendations to the Buryat Council of Ministers, which coopted the right to affirm or veto all allocations of hunting lands. A negative response at any point can be appealed through the court, though the channels to do so remain obscure and untested in Transbaykalia.

Petitioners usually ask for land on which they previously worked or lived: for instance, a group of hunters usually asks for the hunting parcels that individual members of the obshchina were assigned under the sovkhoz system. As noted in Chapter 4, these lands may be those that the hunters' ancestors used prior to the imposition of the kolkhoz systems. Thus, the new obshchina structures may mirror those of the pre-Soviet period. Traditional control of land persisted to some extent even within the context of state disruptions of Evenki territorial patterns: "All the hunting lands have been allotted. Parents with their sons have every one. Then they transfer them to their sons. When the parents die, the sons hunt there. And thus it goes, from generation to generation" (G. A., May 1994).

In other cases, groups ask for land to which their ancestors had no direct ties, but on which they hunted during the Soviet period. Their petitions are an outcome of relocation of families, reallocation of hunting lands, and purges which annihilated or dislocated members of pre-Revolutionary obshchinas. When rich Evenki herders were dispossessed of their herds and lands, other Evenkis eventually assumed tenure of these lands. Working the land to which their parents gained access during the Soviet period, Evenkis have come to know these pastures and hunting allotments and feel they have earned the right to legal protection for continued usage at the very least:

> And now, last year, some [guy] wanted Vova to go away. Vova is working there, my son. I say, it's my own land, it's my hunting allotment. Since 1933…we have worked there always. We fulfilled the plan throughout the 1950s. (E. A., May 1994)

Difficulties arising from historical alienation of lands and occasional contested rights to territory defy easy resolution of petitions.

Since obshchinas for the most part ask for land that their members recently worked, they are making claims to the land holdings of a state enterprise. State enterprises, theoretically under pressure to "de-statize," should not resist these allocations. Some do. *Sovkhozy* and *gospromkhozy* have

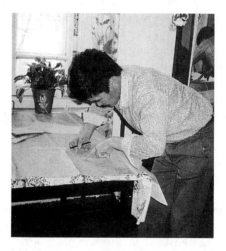

Nikolay Aruneev, Director of an Evenki Reindeer-Herding/Hunting Enterprise, checks a map of Obshchina Lands.

countered the process which erodes their land base by approaching the county government for guaranteed leases over land for a stipulated period of time (e.g., ten years), arguing that they cannot function in the climate of uncertainty brought on by potential reduction of their land base. In some cases such enterprises remain the main suppliers of many services to remote village populations; the county governments, unable to provide such services, have limited bargaining power. Such leases effectively freeze Evenki access to extensive territories, often including the most productive lands.

For instance, an Evenki petitioned for a tract of land north of Lake Oron in the Baunt County, land that would have come from the land base of the Baunt Cooperative Hunting Enterprise (*koopzverpromkhoz*). The enterprise's director protested by threatening to cease supporting the village of Okunëva, on the north shore of the lake. All of Okunëva's supplies and many of its services are paid for by the enterprise, which also is the only employer in town. The director argued that the village, inhabited by a handful of hunters and their families, was unprofitable, especially given the rapidly rising air transport costs (no year-round road connects Okunëva with the outside world). The enterprise would sustain greater losses if the inhabitants could no longer hunt on the lands requested by the Evenki. It could not afford this; it would lay off the state hunters, then withdraw from its role as their supplier (V. M. Imegeev, director of the Baunt Koopzverpromkhoz, 15 July 1994). The county would be left to support this small community, or close it down. Counties, already under serious economic constraints, avoid increasing their fiscal responsibilities; such a threat is enough to hinder or at least stall on the allocation of land to an Evenki obshchina.

Counties establish quantitative norms—so many hectares per hunter or per head of domesticated reindeer—which constrain the obshchina in the size of its requests. It may ask for enough land to support plans for the future: a commune with 100 deer may submit a charter which suggests building the herd to, say, 250 deer, and thus request enough land to pasture the future herd. Norms are allegedly "scientific," that is, based on carrying capacity studies for hunting and reindeer grazing which were carried out during the Soviet period, often several decades ago. These studies are outdated, due to intervening use, fire, and environmental damage. One official noted the poor knowledge of land quality subverts the use of such norms, holding this as the greatest hindrance to equitable land allotment:

> People can ask for so many hectares in a given area, but we don't know the condition of it. There may be a big burn-over, for instance. It may be fair to give one person twice the norm, for instance, if the land is swampy or has burned, whereas another may be able to work well with less than the norm, if it is very rich land, undisturbed. To have, to apply scientific norms, we need good information on land quality. (S. Perfilova, Chairperson of the Severo–Baykal Land Reform Committee, 9 June 1994)

In some counties, individual Evenkis expressed doubts that objectivity in fact played any role. They perceived norms to be applied when convenient, and ignored when they did not fit the political agenda of the county administration.

An obshchina does not own the land allotted to it. It enjoys rights to use the resources it needs to carry out the traditional and nontraditional activities for a period of time stipulated in its charter. In most cases this means that the obshchina has exclusive rights to the game and fur animals, pasture resources, and edible and medicinal plants. "Leases" run from one to twenty-five years, although federal legislation stipulated that such allotments would be permanent, with inheritance rights. In Transbaykalia most "leases" extend for ten years (V. T. Noskov, Buryat Department for Protection of Rational Nature Use of Hunting Resources, 26 July 1994). Initial legislation also stipulated that the land would be used without charge; subsequent legislation has imposed payments.

Evenkis in Transbaykalia began to initiate petitions for allotments almost immediately after a presidential edict called for such allotments. By mid-1994 fifty Evenki obshchinas had been established in Northern Transbaykalia (Table 6.1). Beyond these, a number of petitions awaited action at the county level, or were in various stages of preparation. Most of the extant and planned obshchinas identified hunting as the main traditional activity to be pursued, although over a dozen incorporated reindeer herding as part of the traditional complex of activities. A few near Lake Baykal's northern shore involved harvesting of the lake's seals. The lands so far allocated to Evenki obshchinas constitutes roughly ten percent of the area of Northern Transbaykalia (Figure 6.1).

REFORMS DEFORMED: OBSTACLES TO LAND CLAIMS

Several sets of problems confront Evenkis in their attempts to receive, utilize, and ultimately hold on to land allotments. The problems may be categorized as follows: functional constraints, financial challenges, spatial marginalization, cultural marginalization, competing activities, partial ten-

TABLE 6.1 OBSHCHINAS IN NORTHERN TRANSBAYKALIA

County	# Obshchinas	Hectares (000)
Severo-Baykal	5	395
Muya	1	3
Baunt	1	757
Kalar	8	200
Tungokochen	32	1,104
Tungiro–Olyokma	3	203

Information from: G. S. Balkhanov, Chairperson of Baunt Land Reform Committee, 11 April 1994; V. Ye. Renn, Chairperson of Tungokochen Land Reform Committee, 25 April 1994; G. V. Abramova, President of Association of Numerically Small Peoples of Tungiro–Olëkma County, 12 May 1994; N. N. Buyakov, Chairperson of Kalar Land Reform Committee, 3 June 1994; B. B. Ral'din, Chairperson of Buryat Republic Committee on Land Resources and Planning, 25 July 1994; Records of Severo–Baykal Committee of Land Reform, made available by S. Perfilova, Chairperson, June, July 1994.

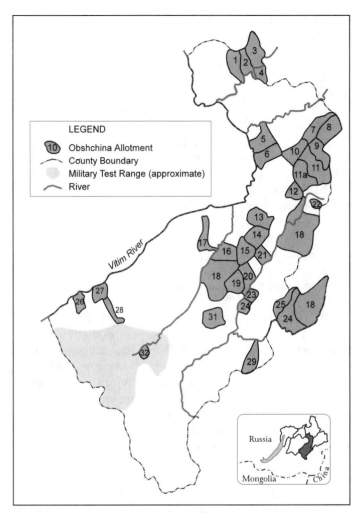

FIGURE 6.1   Obshchina Allotments in Tungokochen County.

ure, and blatant resistance to indigenous land allotments. Together these obstacles severely challenge a land reform process which could potentially provide indigenous people with a significant level of self-governance at the local level.

Functional Constraints:
The Issue of "Tradition"

A presidential edict calls for the transfer of land to obshchinas and families connected with *traditional* activities (O neotlozhnykh 1992). To claim land an indigenous obshchina has to be active in, or willing to return to, traditional activities, as defined by the state. Yet sedentarization and relocation, along with the economic restructuring that occurred during collectivization, forced many indigenous families out of reindeer breeding, and fundamentally changed geographic patterns of other traditional resource usage (e.g., of medicinal and food plants). The transformation of *kolkhozy* into *sovkhozy* coincided with the dispossession of indigenous hunting grounds and the reallocation of these to nonnative hunters. Hunters who have lost their ties to obshchina lands have limited hopes for successfully petitioning for these lands as long as the current hunter remains interested in using them.

Return to traditional activities for many indigenous persons may be difficult for other reasons. Sedentarization has been instrumental in interrupting the transmission of knowledge and skills needed to effectively carry out hunting, herding, and other traditional activities from older to younger generations. Children, spending most of their time in state-run schools with Russian curricula, have failed to come to "know" the lands of their ancestors as intimately as their parents did. Their skills as hunters, trappers, reindeer herders, and processors of the products of these activities do not match those of their grandparents. Today, Evenki children are often literally two or three generations removed from the land. Their grandparents often spent part of their childhood in school, although they returned to traditional activities. Their parents, especially their mothers, often had much less to do with such activities and spent much less time "on the land." Today's adults, especially those currently raising children, may have little expertise regarding traditional activities to share with their offspring. Thus, the very option of returning to traditional activities in order to gain greater control over land is constrained in actual practice.

However, as noted, the worsening economic situation in Russia's North, and the decreasing ability and interest of the state in subsidizing northern populations, may stimulate involvement in subsistence activities. Local stores entertain increasingly empty shelves and local work opportunities in town are contracting. In essence, the traditional activities may enjoy a renaissance born of dire necessity (Pika and Prokhorov 1994).

Financial Challenges

Several Evenki obshchina members cited finances as the single most limiting factor to achieving success in the activities they plan to pursue. Obshchinas demand start-up capital and operational finances. Some obshchina members have received reindeer as part of their "share" when exiting from a state farm. In some areas there are no deer to allocate; persons interested in pursuing an "integrated complex" of traditional activities must rebuild that part of the complex, reindeer husbandry, which was decimated by decades of state neglect and planned phase-outs. In Severo–Baykal County, two Evenki obshchinas choosing to purchase reindeer had to look to the neighboring Kalar County. Reindeer are not cheap; the buyers paid 250,000 rubles per deer (the minimum monthly wage at the time being less than 15,000 rubles). Other needs include transport vehicles (jeeps, snowmobiles, boats), guns and ammunition, radio receivers and transmitters, and, in some cases, funds to pay for helicopter time on a regular basis. The obshchinas need money to pay the wages of their members until they can cover these from fur sales, reindeer meat sales, or other planned products. Moving into a new economic environment in which the *sovkhoz* provides neither supplies and wages nor one's market requires the establishment of new relationships for buying goods and selling products. In Transbaykalia some hunters contract back to the state enterprises to sell their furs and buy their supplies from these concerns—essentially working as private contractors to the farms. In Tungokochen County fourteen obshchinas united in a shareholder's association, using this vehicle to deal with provisioning and sales of products. The association also hired a bookkeeper to provide some of the services which the *sovkhoz* would have previously taken care of.

The Russian Federation's Committee on Northern Development (*Goskomsever*) has provided some capital, in terms of both grants and loans on favorable terms. Its budget, however, is limited. Bank loans can also be applied for. The economic crisis plaguing Russia has wreaked havoc with the system to financially support obshchinas. With rapid inflation and a grinding bureaucracy, amounts applied for and granted by the State have often been worth little by the time they reach the recipients. Bank loans have involved high rates of interest to protect against inflation (e.g., two hundred and twelve percent in the summer of 1994 in Buryatia), and relatively short periods for pay back. The periods are rarely long enough to allow an obshchina time to develop products and markets for these, a problem increased by bureaucratic inefficiencies. As one Evenki obshchina head lamented:

> I lost two years in trying to get these reindeer, due to idiotic politics, mainly at the county level.... Losing two years means that in three years I will already need to start producing meat, to pay back the loans. At 212%! Yes, I get five years before payments are due, but I've already lost two. (Yu. Chernoev, 3 August 1994)

Financial constraints may explain the relatively high percentage of pensioners involved in the obshchina movement.

> On the whole it's mainly pensioners here [who join the obshchinas]...and invalids. Pensioners at least live on their pensions, but those who would work without money, well, they need to live. (I. D., April 1994)

Without assured wages, and without sufficient start-up capital to weather the interval required in which to start production and find markets, many Evenkis feel that they cannot afford to abandon a waged job, even a low-paid one, for the new opportunity of developing one's own business.

High unemployment among the Evenki population in Northern Transbaykalia, however, has mitigated this concern. Legislation initially stipulated that there would be no charge for lands allotted to indigenous obshchinas for traditional use. A 1993 decree contravened these previous acts, calling for payment to the Forest Service for the use of land for hunting and pasturing. The decree provoked heated debate. Some members of the Forest Service deemed that it held ultimate rights to and responsibilities for the flora of lands under its aegis. As fur bearing animals and reindeer depended on this flora and potentially degraded it, the users of such animals should pay a land rent (A. Goloushkin, head of the Buryat Republic Forest Service, 25 July 1994). Many outside the Forest Service felt that it had overstepped its bounds by essentially laying claim to everything alive in the forests:

> The Forest Service seems to think it has the right to charge. What right does it have to the animals? Animals, the fauna, was always ours. The Forest Service has the right to trees. The forest isn't ours, but the animals and birds are. The Forest Service didn't raise these animals. (V. M. Imgeev, 15 July 1994)

Others would find bemusing the idea that hunting enterprises are anymore the rightful owners of the fauna than the Forest Service!

Within Northern Transbaykalia, the response to such charges differed. In Chita Province, the decree seems to be accepted as fact, applicable to Evenki obshchinas as well as to state enterprises. The province executed the decree by devolving implementation to each county. In terms of charges to obshchinas, Kalar County has levied payment per number of reindeer pastured, or a percentage of earnings from hunting. Tungokochen and Tungiro–Olëkma Counties have calculated charges per hectare allotted to an obshchina (N. N. Buyakov, Chairperson, Kalar County Land Reform Committee, 3 June 1994).

In Buryatia, while officials disagreed on the merit of the decree, all generally agreed that Evenki obshchinas would be exempt. After setting a rate of sixteen rubles per hectare, the Buryat Government passed its own decree, allowing certain land-users not to pay until the issue was further considered. Further, since a new parliament was to be elected in mid-1994, the Buryat Government postponed the activation of the federal decree until this parliament could discuss its equability. Many officials, including Forest Service employees, shrugged off the decree as unrealistic:

> Only prospectors and gold miners can afford to pay. The *gospromkhozy*, the *sovkhozy* and the *koopzverpromkhozy* simply don't have the money....Of course the Forest Service would like to be paid. We [the county Forest Service office] would be able to keep seventy percent, and turn over thirty percent to [the republican level Forest Service]. But if there is no money, it's no use asking for it. [To do so] would send these organizations into bankruptcy. (A. V. Solov'ev, Director, Bagdarin Forest Service, 18 July 1994)

The state enterprise directors concur, and at least in one county (Baunt) have been backed by the administration:

> The Forest Service wants to charge for land. It wants to charge 16 rubles per hectare. Sure, that seems like a pittance. But given the land we have, it would be 37 million rubles a year for us! Thirty million for the *gospromkhoz*. Twenty million for *Yukte* [a local cooperative reindeer-herding enterprise]. We refused to pay and Khingelov [the county chairperson] has supported us in this. (V. M. Imgeev, 15 July 1994)

Many Evenkis involved in the obshchina movement fear that where (or if) such a fee is strictly imposed, it will subvert obshchinas' attempts to create economically viable operations.

Spatial Marginalization

Evenki obshchinas must petition the county government for a land allotment. While the procedure described above seems straightforward, it poses a number of challenges to the petitioner. First, many villages lie at a distance from the county center (Figure 1.1). Ground transport is often limited to winter months, when the ground is frozen, as all-weather road networks are poorly developed. If no navigable waterway exists, air transport remains the only alternative for a significant part of the year. Skyrocketing transportation costs, especially in the air sector, have brought on the virtual collapse of regular air service to outlying villages. Flights that were once scheduled several times per week may occur bi-weekly, with luck.

Even if a flight is available, a potential petitioner from an outlying village may be unable to afford to travel to the county center. A return air fare from village to county center in 1994 often exceeded villagers' monthly income. Lack of reliable telephone and telegraph communications with the center further thwart a petitioner's attempts to affirm whether government officials with whom he or she must meet will be present during the visit. Evenki petitioners related several cases in which they had made trips only to find key officials gone for several days.

If problems are encountered with one's petition for an obshchina land allotment at the county level, one may need to reach beyond the county capital, to the "center." Heads of newly formed obshchinas whose petitions have languished at the local level for a variety of reasons, or have failed to receive promised finances, have traveled to Ulan–Ude and Chita, and even Moscow, to try to force action. These trips are expensive, in terms of time, money, and psychological stress. As one petitioner for an obshchina lamented:

> In December I lived in Ulan–Ude for two weeks, I talked to everyone, I resolved things with [the president of the republican-level Evenki Association]. But the documents have lain in Moscow since December, and now we can't get credit. I need to go there, but how will I go? I don't know anyone there. You don't need to know Ulan–Ude, but it's a different city, Moscow is. There you need to know the language, and you need money. I estimated that it

would take about a half-million [rubles]. The plane is expensive for one person, and, well, you really need to go with someone else. (I. D., April 1994)

Modifications to laws and passage of new legislation have required that obshchina petitions under consideration be correspondingly modified and in some cases, that existing obshchinas reregister. Lack of information about this can penalize a process, another outcome of spatial marginalization. And even when Evenki obshchina members receive timely information that action is required, they may judge it too expensive to attempt. With no assurance that the right persons will be in place to sign and stamp forms, the trip to submit a petition, to modify it, to reregister, or simply to follow up on the progress of an application, can be an extremely expensive gamble. For the spatially marginalized, if monitoring the progress of one's petition through the bureaucracy remains critical, it often is also unfeasible.

The legislation which required fees paid to the Forest Service, mentioned earlier, further heightened the problems of spatial marginalization where it was implemented. In cases where an allotment straddles two Forest Service districts, the obshchina must now work out of two centers, registering paper work and maps and making payments at the centers of both. For instance, in the Kalar County, N. D. Danilova's obshchina must deal with both the Charskiy Forest Service District Office in Staraya Chara, and the Nelyatskiy office in Nelyati (E. Borisenko, head of the Charskiy Forest Service, 7 June 1994). This costs Danilova in both time and money.

Finally, the reaction of state enterprise officials to the process of obshchina land allotments underscores the problems of spatial marginalization. In Chita Province in at least one case a state farm quickly negotiated a ten-year renewal on its lease, freezing petitions by Evenkis to the lands it held.

Whoever managed in time got land.... And before the Evenkis got to it, all the land had already been allotted...it should have been the other way around, the Russians requesting the land, but now to the contrary, it's the Evenkis who from time immemorial lived here, who have to go [asking for land]. (N. A., May 1994)

More conversant with administrative processes, better connected to officials in the centers, and enjoying greater access to the center, the *sovkhoz* director beat his challengers to the table, and secured the best of the offerings.

Cultural Marginalization

When asked why one state hunter had not received a land allocation for an obshchina which he had pursued for three years, Baunt County's Land Reform Committee chairperson answered that part of the problem was this person's lack of persistence in pushing his case (G. Balkhanov, 18 April 1994). He had only been by the office once or twice and had not pursued his petition diligently. That the hunter lived in an outlying village, not connected by road, when not on his state hunting plot yet another some 150 kilometers beyond the village—and thus would be hard pressed to follow up on his petition—seemingly failed to receive consideration. Yet, while spatial marginalization may have played a significant role in the hunter's perceived passivity, cultural norms also appear to subvert the process of gaining land allotments for obshchinas.

We're not demanding by nature. We don't push our agenda. Perhaps a "no" is really a "maybe" from a Russian, but we accept it as a "no." (D. M., April 1994)

Evenkis are required to deal with governmental structures on Russian terms and turf. A combination of state paternalism and domination has fostered an attitude of dependency and submissiveness among indigenous northerners in Russia, a situation which Native leaders abhor as one of the most damaging legacies of Soviet nationality policy as directed at northern peoples.

Evenki women suggested an interesting gender dimension to the issue of cultural passivity. One noted that her own success in obtaining land allotments (as well as other achievements) hinged on shedding cultural mores that many Evenkis retained, mores that constrain an aggressive approach to realization of one's rights. Earlier removed from traditional activities, sedentarized in villages, and acculturated, more completely incorporated into the Russian educational system, Evenki women have learned more of the skills for dealing with Russian officials on their terms. They have cast off some of the cultural reluctance to challenge authorities.

> If a man asks for land and is told "no," that's it. He accepts the "no," maybe goes off [drinking (indicated by a fillip to the neck)]. A woman doesn't accept "no" as an answer. She'll ask again, or ask someone else, until she gets it. (G. R., August 1994)

The woman quoted, when told "no" at the county level, proceeded through "nos" at higher levels, until finally receiving a "yes" in Moscow to her request for an obshchina allotment and financial support. Although the emphasis on traditional activities disadvantages women in receiving land allotments, the requirement of meeting of Russian bureaucratic procedures may at times handicap the less acculturated part of the Evenki population, the males working in traditional fields.

This in fact is one reason why Evenki women have come to predominate in the leadership of at least the lower (township and county) levels of indigenous associations. In 1994, of the six county-level Evenki associations, four were headed by women. From its inception until 1995 a woman served as head of the Chita provincial Evenki Association. Several of these women lamented the fact that, as female, their opinions appeared to carry less weight with provincial, republican, and federal officials. The dilemma is palpable: Evenki women are often better positioned to negotiate on Russian terms, but still less accepted as rightful representatives of their people by sexist officials.

Simultaneous Land Initiatives

One Evenki individual who petitioned for an obshchina allotment ran into difficulty because the boundary of the allotment coincides with the boundary of the township in which it is located. This imaginary line also constitutes the boundary of Baunt County. The township had previously sought to change its status from a nonethnic township to an Evenki township. To do so requires the confirmation of its boundaries. This petitioner's problems were rooted in the fact that Baunt County has a boundary dispute with the neighboring Muya County (Fondahl 1996). Until the boundary dispute between counties was resolved, the boundaries of the "new" Evenki township could not be confirmed; until the township's boundaries were confirmed, the petitioner's allotment's boundaries could not be confirmed. Until his allotment's boundaries were confirmed, the petitioner and his obshchina could not begin activities on this land. Several of the members of his obshchina were un- or underemployed and wished to begin hunting and haying on the land; he talked of reintroducing reindeer to this allotment as well. As prices increase, his chances for obtaining sufficient capital which will support the obshchina's initial development grew dimmer, as did the hopes and aspirations (and attendant energies) of the obshchina's members.

Throughout the Russian North, the obshchina movement proceeds simultaneously with other land initiatives. In some cases such initiatives can ensure a more secure future for obshchinas. For instance, obshchinas finding themselves encapsulated within newly established protected zones for traditional activities (see Chapter 7) enjoy added protection against environmental threats that might undercut their ability to pursue traditional activities. In other instances, changes in boundaries, tenure status, or use designation can obstruct petitions for obshchina allotments. Legislation has failed in most cases to stipulate the resolution of such potential conflicts, leaving Evenkis at the mercy of county and provincial/republican officials in many cases.

Environmental Threats

If financial constraints present a significant obstacle to initiating obshchinas, environmental threats hinder their continued viability. Indigenous obshchinas receive exclusive use rights to some of the fauna and flora on the land allotted to them. They do not receive use rights to the subsurface resources, the timber resources (though they may cut for subsistence needs), airspace, and so forth. Ministries and their departments at various levels (federal, republican/ provincial, county) continue to hold the rights to these resources. Legislation fails to provide comprehensive protection against exploration of such resources, except when an obshchina's land allotment falls within a protected zone. Nontraditional activities can affect an obshchina's ability to continue using its land in fundamental ways. In Northern Transbaykalia, in the most extraordinary case, Kim Garpaneev's obshchina received a land allotment within a military testing ground (Figure 6.1, allotment 32). Obshchina members are restricted to visiting the land during a short period in mid-winter, and need special permission to enter and exit the land on each occasion of movement. These provisions, imposed to ensure the safety of the obshchina members, severely compromise the level of self-determination this obshchina enjoys (Aruneev 1992).

Missiles exploded on the testing ground frequently set fire to the tayga, decimating sizable areas of hunting lands, both inside and outside of its boundaries. While lightening and other natural causes also set fires, locals identify anthropogenic sources—missiles, reconnaissance geologists, miners, sports hunters, and poachers—as much more significant sources of the forest fires which have destroyed large tracts of reindeer pasture and hunting habitat. The head of one obshchina estimated that thirty percent of his obshchina's land, and over seventy percent of the land in northern Tungokochen County as a whole, had been burned over in the last two decades. Without significant state intervention, he can only assume that such fires will continue (N. A., May 1994). Obshchina allotment boundaries, as mapped by the state, suggest much less flexibility than their prerevolutionary predecessors. Will traditional mechanisms for dealing with such exigencies, including a flexibility of tenure and territoriality, be revived? How can such flexibility be encouraged, given state interests in rigid bounding of property?

In the gold-rich environment of Northern Transbaykalia, mining poses threats to Evenki obshchinas, beyond those of forest fires started by careless miners. Upstart mining guilds pepper the tayga, exploiting new sites, and reworking old, formerly unprofitable ones with new technology. Faced with a crisis economic situation, county and republican/ provincial governments are unlikely to consider the needs of the herder/hunter over the miner, and *at best* try to occasionally enforce legislation requiring as environmentally sensitive means of extraction as possible and remuneration for damage done. Damage however is not restricted to the mining nodes. Tailings and processing chemicals pollute water sources. Roads destroy swaths of fragile tayga (exacerbated by the fact that discontinuous permafrost underlies a substantial portion of Northern Transbaykalia). Roads also give access to poachers who neither differentiate the domestic reindeer from its wild counterpart nor recognize the borders of newly established obshchinas.

Now, see, there are many prospecting guilds, prospectors, they are mining gold, and they cover practically the whole regions, they've divided up every stream between themselves, they fight between themselves for plots. In short all the rivers are now divvied up This is it for the fish and the animals. (P. K., April 1994)

BuryatGold has a plan, as previously. They have a plan for [mining] gold in the [Baunt] County, except that now it's been increased by 1.5 times...and no one there is going to worry about the ecology. Two years ago ecology arose on the scene, but now it's all been forgotten, now money is needed. Everyone has forgotten about this matter. (V. T., April 1994)

In the Baunt County, the administration in one case granted a gold mining license to the obshchina on whose land allotment a lode is situated:

The head of the administration met us on this one. There were seven competitors, seven powerful firms wanting to work the deposit. We have practically no machinery, no money. But the head of the administration ordered that the people who live in Ust–Dzhilinda take the license themselves, and then find investors. (A. T., April 1994)

This obshchina's land allotment, unlike others in Northern Transbaykalia, incorporates an entire Evenki township (Ust–Dzhilinda). The granting of such a license caused much debate: some of the county's inhabitants feel that obshchinas should receive land for *traditional* activities, and while a modicum of nontraditional development is acceptable, gold-mining is way beyond the limits of what federal legislation envisaged. Proponents of this view see the Evenkis as using legislation meant to protect their cultural uniqueness to make an unfair grab for resources. Countering this argument, the head of the obshchina which received the right to the deposit contended that his interests in gold-mining were two-fold: to improve the general standard, very low at present, of the members of the obshchina (in this case a whole village), and to revive, by means of capitalization provided by the gold, the traditional fields of hunting and reindeer herding. Moreover, obshchina control, he argued, suggests greater likelihood of following environmental regulations and protecting the environment to a greater extent than outsiders might. Another person echoed his views:

> If I'm standing around someone else's office, I might think nothing of spitting on the floor. It's the cleaning woman's job to clean it, it's not my floor. But would I ever think of spitting on the floor of my own home? If a person controls the land, he will take care of it. (E. B., June 1994)

Forestry operations pose threats similar to those posed by gold mining to newly created obshchinas, in that the county and higher governments see such operations as a vital source of income and refuse to recognize that operations *near* to allotments may wreak havoc on the potential of traditional activities planned by that obshchina. Logging roads, as well as logged areas, modify game and fur animal distribution, as well as serving as conduits for poachers. It is not only the cutting of timber, but also the poaching, fire danger, and destruction of the soil by vehicles that caused Evenkis to protest forestry operations.

The future of obshchinas also may hinge on the future of other industrial projects: in Tungokochen County, for instance, parts of two allocations (Figure 6.1, Allotments 5, 6) may end up under water if a long-debated hydroelectric project is built. While the fate of this project is uncertain, its potential was great enough to warrant exclusion of land in the projected flood basin from a "territory of traditional nature use" set up in the Tungokochen County (V. Ye. Renn, chairperson of the Tungokochen County Committee on Land Reform, 25 April 1994; see Chapter 7).

Resistance to Reforms

If legislative reform can address some of the uncertainties facing obshchinas vis-a-vis competition from industrial and associated activities, another sort of partial tenure confounds some Evenk individuals' attempts to pursue exactly what federal legislation (O neotlozhnykh 1992) promotes: the "*integrated* use" of reindeer pasture, hunting, fishing, and other lands, for the revival of traditional cultural-economic activities. In the tayga no single activity (hunting, fishing, or reindeer herding) traditionally sustained a family, obshchina or clan; rather, a combination of these activities provided for both subsistence and commercial/trade needs. Federal acts have recognized this; so have some regional officials who oppose what they perceive as "privatization" of land. Understanding the criticality of an "integrated" approach, they have attempted to undermine the obshchina movement by consciously awarding more limited usufruct rights than laws currently provide for.

Witness the case of Yu. I. Chernoev, of the Severo–Baykal County, director of the "Uluki" (Squirrel) obshchina. Chernoev fought to receive a parcel of land on which he could help revitalize reindeer herding, which had been almost fully decimated in the county. Domesticated reindeer numbered over 2000 in the mid-1970s, but had dropped to well

Valentina and Yuri Chernoev on their Obshchina territory.

under 100 animals by 1992 (A. M. Alekseev, Chairperson of Kindigir Evenki Township, June 1992; V. S. Karatinsky, director of Uoyanskiy Gospromkoz, June 1992). Chernoev originally worked as a herder himself when a herding operation still existed in his area. When herding was liquidated he took up a job as a hunter. When the possibility of "becoming one's own boss" appeared, he launched a plan to purchase deer, and set up an obshchina operation that would herd, hunt, collect edible and medicinal plants, and perhaps eventually develop ethno-eco-tourism (Yu. Chernoev, June 1992 and August 1994).

After a sustained struggle with the county government, Chernoev was granted rights to deer pasture over some 223 thousand hectares. However, he received hunting rights only to the northern part of this parcel. The county government then gave another obshchina, "Oron," the rights to hunt on part of the southern portion of Chernoev's pasture allotment. Using a typical "divide-and-rule" strategy that states often employ against indigenous peoples encapsulated within their boundaries (Nietschmann 1994), a local government intensely resistant to indigenous land rights successfully incited dissension between the two Evenki obshchinas. In this escalating conflict each side has threatened to use arms against "trespassers" on their allotted lands (Mazholis *et al.* 1994; interview with "Oron" members, August 1994). The county government can now point to this case as exemplary of what may ensue when land rights are granted to "feuding natives;" other Evenkis in the area petition for obshchina allotments against this backdrop.[2]

When allotments of partial tenure failed to quaff indigenous ambitions, more blatant tactics were used. The "Vozrozhdenie" (Rebirth) obshchina was finally awarded an allotment of land, if with partial usage rights, after two years of struggling, taking that struggle all the way to Moscow. Obshchina members began to build a homestead, using an abandoned Forest Service shed located on the property while construction proceeded. This building, if modest, served as shelter—until Forest Service personnel burnt it down. The Forest Service claimed that the building belonged to it, and thus it had the right to dispose of it. Members of "Vozhrozhdenie" viewed this act as obstructionist tactics to establishing the obshchina, and claimed that the Forest Service had also attacked a bathhouse that

---

2. Other victims of the "partial tenure" strategy in the Severo–Baykal County include the obshchinas "Vozrozhdenie," and "Kedr," both of which obtained herding rights without hunting rights. "Vozrozhdenie" eventually received hunting rights to an allotment of 23,700 hectares (G. Rogova, letter to the author, 3 April 1995).

   One obshchina, "Kingilan" (Tungokochen County), also received pasture rights without hunting rights, to 14,346 hectares of land. This was explained as a problem of timing—the members applied for lands prior to provincial recognition of federal legislation requiring the support of integrated activities. While the *gospromkhoz* maintained hunting rights over the pasture land allotted to this obshchina, the obshchina later received another allotment for hunting on lands where its head had formerly worked as a state hunter.

   My evaluation of the situation in Severo–Baykal County in no way is meant as a criticism of the chairperson of the Committee on Land Reform, S. Perfilova, who, sincerely disturbed by the machinations of other members of the county government, sought a solution to the impasse created.

they were constructing. No compensation, or even reprimand by the county government to the local division of the Forest Service was forthcoming (G. Rogova, August 1994). Use of such tactics is not limited to official bodies and their personnel:

> Hunters have started to set fires especially, so that the Evenkis don't demand these lands...[the hunters] need hunting lands but they don't need reindeer pasture. They make fires, and that's it for the lichens, nothing more grows there. (N. A., May 1994)

LIMITATIONS

A half-century of state-orchestrated land alienations complicated, rather than erased, a sense of rights to certain territories, rights based on predecessors' use and occupancy. The numerous petitions for obshchina lands speak to Evenki desires to enjoy territorial recognition. Russian legislation which grants obshchinas the right to receive land allotments for the pursuance of "traditional" activities can be seen as a positive, if small step, toward effecting greater self-governance, as called for under international conventions on indigenous rights. Limitations to this approach are found both in its current implementation and its future prospects. Disintegrating (or nonexistent) transportation and communications infrastructure complicates Evenki attempts to gain land allotments, as do cultural norms which seventy years of Soviet power failed to eradicate or even strengthened. Federal legislation provides neither adequate protection against geographically proximate industrial activities which threaten traditional activities, nor against local officials who pervert such legislation in order to stymie devolution of power beyond their control.

While obshchinas explicitly acknowledge pre-Soviet indigenous land tenure structures, they fail to replicate them wholly. Communal control has been preserved to some extent in a period of concerted individualization. However, the strict bounding of space, usually along state-delineated hunting borders, refutes the flexibility of resource use and land tenure of old. One Evenki, a former herder, worried about the eventual consequences of allotments of 25,000 or even 250,000 hectares: "Naturally, to put reindeer with their master in such a cage will bring nothing but the death of the deer" (N. A., August 1995). Will Evenki groups will be able to work themselves to overcome or ignore state-drawn boundaries where these hinder the health of traditional activities?

Most critically, the new obshchinas allow Evenkis to enjoy communal use rights, but not ownership:

> It's not our land, but more precisely, only our hunting grounds. Land and hunting grounds are two different things. That is, if it were our land, everything would be a lot simpler. We would be like masters....but as it is now we can only carry out the hunt. (P. S., April 1994)

The land remains federal property. And self-determination over obshchina lands thus remains but partial.

7

Gaining Ground? First Steps and Future Needs

OTHER APPROACHES TO EVENKI LAND RIGHTS

If the move to (re-)create obshchina territories acknowledges the traditional land tenure mechanisms of indigenous peoples, its realization in Transbaykalia gives Evenki obshchinas partial control over an archipelago of land allotments. As noted in Chapter 6, these lands lie vulnerable to outside influences: environmental degradation of the surrounding areas and land uses that threaten the activities which the obshchina has chosen to pursue. The importance of obtaining the rights to communal use of, and control over, obshchina lands, while undeniable, still leaves Evenkis who are interested in pursuing traditional activities poorly protected.

Two other approaches to improving Evenki rights to controlling activities in their homeland merit brief mention. First, recent legislation has allowed the creation of native townships and counties, the latter similar to those created in the 1920s and 1930s (Chapter 4). As the Russian Federation devolves power to lower levels, the ability for townships and counties to effect greater local control over decision making has grown. Invested in local governments at the county and township level is greater control over resource development and environmental protection. Concomitant with this devolution of power is the ability of indigenous peoples to create "native" townships and "native" counties, thus creating loci of native self-government.

Four of the townships in the Severo–Baykal and Baunt Counties have become "Evenki Townships" under this new legislation (O svobodnom 1990; Ob obrazovanii 1991), and one county has declared itself an "Evenki County." Evenki proponents of such administrative units see these "native" townships and counties as giving further protective capabilities to the obshchina lands. Local governments could guard against activities which pose threats to obshchina lands. Moreover, as such native units are supposed to receive additional funding directly from the federal government, some Evenkis and non-Evenkis saw the creation of such "Evenki" units as a strategic move financially.

However, Evenkis constitute a minority in the so-called "Evenki Townships" of Baunt and Severo–Baykal Counties, and a small fraction of the total population of these two counties. Thus, as democracy gains strength in the Russian Federation, the ability of Evenkis to influence decisions which would ensure a continuing improvement in their ability to use and enjoy their traditional lands may actually deteriorate. The "Evenki Townships" and counties may prove fictive *native* administrations, with nonnatives predominating in the administration of these territories.

In Chita Province, while neither Evenki townships nor Evenki counties have been established, a strong Evenki contingent lobbied for the restoration of the Vitim–Olëkma National District (1930–1938), through editorial letters to county- and provincial-level newspapers, through released statements to the federal government, and even through a demonstration in front of the provincial capital's governmental buildings. Their demands fell on deaf ears.

The other legislative initiative to improving Evenki rights to controlling activities in their homeland takes a decidedly different approach. It allows for the establishment of protected areas, in which nontraditional activities are prohibited or strictly controlled. Such legislation (O neotlozhnykh 1992) calls for setting aside large territories for these activities. Obshchina lands located within such territories are afforded extra protection against the effects of noncompatible land uses on neighboring plots. At the same time, Evenki obshchina members may be constrained in the breadth of activities they choose to pursue if their obshchina territory does fall within such a protected territory. Baunt County established "Evenki reserve zones" by early 1992. In the three northern counties of the Chita Province, protected areas known as "Territories of Traditional Nature Use" (Figure 7.1), constituting twenty-seven percent of the counties' total territory, were set up in 1994 (Mikheev 1995). Most Evenkis applaud the concept of protecting larger territories from industrial encroachment through such protected areas. Yet heated debate stemmed from the limited opportunities Evenkis had to participate in land selection for these protected areas. Moreover, Evenkis worry that, in that land can be removed from the "Territories of Traditional Nature Use" by referendum, that provincial authorities will misinterpret federal legislation by allowing all residents to participate in such referendums, rather than just the indigenous population. Chita Province, in creating the "Territories of Traditional Nature Use," explicitly underscored that such protected territories did not give special rights to the indigenous population, but instead protected the land base needed for the continuation of traditional activities as pursued by the Evenkis but also many nonnative persons. In fact, nonnative hunters outnumber Evenki hunters, a fact not lost on a provincial government worried about "ethnic tensions." Protected areas, envisioned in federal legislation as "native reserve areas" have, in the Chita Province, assumed more a role of environmental protection against industrial activities that threaten traditional ones than a role of rectifying Evenki control over homelands. Evenki rights to land, if improved on paper, are still ambiguous and fragile in practice.

TRADITIONAL ACTIVITIES, LAND, AND THE NEXT GENERATION

If we were to revisit the imaginary family of Basuk and Tyan a hundred years after her birth, we might find an aged Anna, twice widowed (one husband lost to World War II,

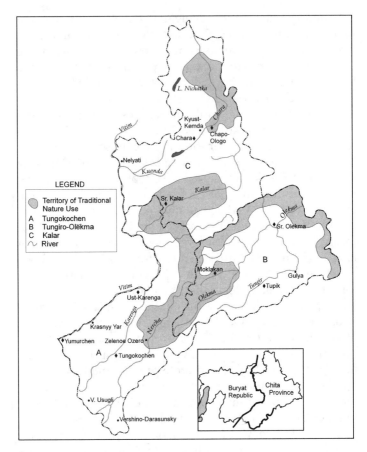

FIGURE 7.1 Territories of traditional nature use in Chita Province.

another to an alcohol-related accident), who had long ago been induced to settle down in a village and take up a Russian occupation, who had given birth to her children in a small village hospital, and who had lost all contact with the lands she enjoyed during her childhood and those she had begun to know in the early years of her first marriage. Her daughters, adults and perhaps even young grandparents in the late 1990s, would have spent much of their lives in the village. Her sons may have continued traditional activities as a profession, and lived apart from their children, who would have attended boarding schools and learned Russian ways. Anna may have lamented at how her sons never achieved the level of skill of her father, or even her husbands, in hunting and caring for deer. She may have pondered on her own life: she enjoyed the comforts of village life—the bathhouse, the clinic, the library, the (rather empty) shop—although these seemed meager to those she saw available in other parts of Russia and the world, from the grainy screen of her black and white TV. In fact, she could use her TV with decreasing regularity these days, as her village's faltering ability to buy diesel undermined its ability to provide electricity. She also missed the freedom of life in the tayga, the relatively more equal role of women which she thought her mom and grandma enjoyed, the clean environment, the fresh country diet rich in meat. Remembering the early years of her life, when she helped her mother pack and drive the reindeer from camp to camp, she may have lamented the precipitous decline in reindeer numbers.

Life has changed dramatically for the Evenkis of Transbaykalia over the course of the twentieth century. Most Evenkis view these changes as incorporating both positive and negative features. Very few, if any, wish to return to a lifestyle similar to those of their ancestors living at the beginning of the twentieth century. Substantially more would like to pursue the traditional activities of their ancestors, in a modernized fashion which incorporates appropriate contemporary technology with traditional systems of social exchange and self-governance.

Can an emphasis on traditional activities as the basis for indigenous land reforms accord with the needs of today's Evenkis? Many Evenkis feel that, indeed, it can contribute substantially to their cultural persistence. But the reforms must proceed hand-in-hand with a reeducation of Evenki youth, a reaffirmation of the cultural values of their ancestors, and a reintroduction to the land-based activities which embodied these values. In offering such, Evenki leaders argue, they offer their children a genuine chance to choose between traditional and nontraditional activities, or to choose a life which combines the two.

To this end, Evenki cultural leaders have initiated "back-to-the-land" training for both Evenki and other local children. In Bagdarin (Baunt County), an Evenki Cultural Center founded by Darya Mironova in the early 1990s offers after-school lessons in Evenki language and arts (skin processing, sewing, beading, and traditional tool making). In 1994 the Center opened up a field school, on a small land allotment provided by the county administration; on this land children learn to track, trap, and live in the forest. In Tungokochen County, Evenki culture camps in the early 1990s offered children from the villages a chance to live for a few weeks in the forest near the camp of a reindeer herder, to observe herding and hunting first hand, and to try their hand at some of the elementary skills required of hunters and herders. In Severo–Baykal County, the school in village of Kholodnaya has opened up a field camp similar to that of Baunt County. Victor Ganyugin has introduced a group of boys in ski, snowshoe and backboard making, fishing and sealing techniques, and hunting and herding skills. The group spends a few

Victor Ganyugin, teacher of Evenki Culture Class, and his students.

weeks in the summer on his obshchina territory, experiencing first hand the work required in these activities. The initiators of these field schools emphasize the need to involve both Evenki and non-Evenki children. While aimed at Evenki cultural persistence, the schools open the eye of non-Evenki to the importance of Evenki activities, for Evenki and for the population as a whole of the Transbaykalia countryside. Mironova and Ganyugin note that more likely than not it will be the non-Evenkis who continue to predominate in the administrative and economic structures that influence to so great a degree Evenki life; by offering a better understanding of Evenki cultural values to these children as well as Evenkis, the field schools and cultural centers may contribute to a future generation of decision makers more accommodating of Evenki values.

Individual efforts parallel those of the cultural centers. In a number of cases Evenki boys who have run afoul of the legal system have been "adopted" by Evenki obshchinas and removed to "the bush." Adoption, long recognized in Evenki culture as a social response to the needs of both orphaned children and childless families, has taken on a new role of dual rehabilitation—rehabilitation for young miscreants concomitant with rehabilitation for traditional activities. Often effectively orphaned, a few children have begun to commit acts of "hooliganism"—petty but escalating crime. They drop out of school in their early teens or even before. Their future appears grim. Removed to distant obshchina lands, these boys receive training in the skills of herder or hunter. The few young men with whom I talked who had experienced such "adoption" found the new life in the bush invigorating and considered themselves rescued from an unpromising future. They missed TV and the occasional village dance, but held that they would not chose to return to the village-based life they had led. Yesterday's delinquents may become some of the leading figures in tomorrow's land-based traditional activities.

Evenki movements thus are addressing the retraining of youth (especially boys) to better afford them the opportunity to pursue traditional activities if that is what they wish. These efforts articulate well with, and are a natural partner to, land reform based on traditional activities. If traditional activities themselves have receded in economic importance over the last few decades, their cultural significance for Evenkis remains paramount. Moreover, in the rocky transition toward a market economy, their economic importance increases anew.

EVENKI GOALS FOR INDIGENOUS LAND REFORM: PARTIAL FULFILLMENT

Regaining control over enough of their lands to ensure cultural survival remains a cardinal goal of Evenkis in Northern Transbaykalia. The territorial requisites of their traditional activities have been challenged by decades of disruption by the state—sedentarization, forced relocation, land enclosures, alienations, and reallocations. That recent legislation openly implicates past policy as grievously mistaken vindicates Evenki struggles to maintain or regain control of their homelands.

Many Evenkis thus looked at the initial moves toward indigenous land reform with guarded optimism. That special provisions were created for the northern regions, allowing for communal control over land (obshchina allotments) in the face of widespread pressures for "privatization," suggested the state's willingness to listen to indigenous demands. The renewal of the possibility for native forms of self-governance, such as Evenki townships and Evenki counties, implied a new nationality policy sensitive to the needs of small-numbered peoples. Protection for large tracts of land critical to traditional activities, through the creation of "Territories of Traditional Nature Use," offered hopes for containing the industrial expansion which has degraded so much of the pasture lands, hunting and fishing grounds, and gathering sites of the indigenous population.

Yet state reforms have failed to satisfy Evenki aspirations, both in letter and in implementation. Of course Evenki opinions differ on the direction reforms should take. Many persons view the obshchinas as an appropriate locus of self-governance; the main problem with these lies in the hindrances created by county officials to their allocation, and in insufficient finances to kick-start their operations. Others see obshchinas as a new form of land enclosure that fails to recognized fully the flexibility, as well as communality, of land tenure which underpinned Evenki traditional activities. They voice concerns about the obshchina allotments fostering competition, rather than unity, among Evenki communities. Evenkis themselves have played a very limited role in determining the nature, size, location, and configuration of allotments. Acknowledging pre-Soviet territoriality and tenure patterns of indigenous peoples, today's obshchina territories are mapped along Soviet boundaries by (barely post-Soviet) authorities.

The newly created Evenki townships and counties also meet Evenki aspirations only partly. Is an Evenki township in which Evenkis constitute only twenty-five percent of the population, and hold an even smaller percent of official posts a true locus of native self-government? Or is it a pretty façade for public consumption, all the more damaging, because it appears that "something has been done"? Can this reform be pushed farther to require a guaranteed level of native representation in decision-making fora? The initial euphoria over ability to establish such Evenki territorial units has, for some, faded into a tired resentment. The moniker "Evenki" in front of the township or county may bring the occasional federal ruble, but the chance that it will specifically aid native self-determination appears slight.

Protected areas, too, seemed a promising means of ensuring a future for Evenki traditional activities and thus Evenki identity. Yet their implementation has been riddled, from the viewpoint of many Evenkis, by inadequacies, in terms of expanse, in terms of what is protected, and in terms of the potential for land alienation.

The constant struggle to both challenge the limits of federal legislation and to push local implementation to approach those limits has thus tempered optimism. The Evenkis of Northern Transbaykalia live in a nested political geography of township, county, republic/province, and federal state. Relations toward and goals characterizing indigenous land reforms vary by level. Reforms orchestrated mainly in Moscow are reformatted by Buryat Republican legislation or Chita Province rules, in accordance with views shared by officials at those intermediate levels of power. Many are implemented by more-or-less willing officials at the county level. The goals of these players, not only as individuals, but also as representatives of different levels of power with different agendas, vary. With the disintegration of Soviet power has come the devolution of power, a process in which federal officials participate with mixed emotions. Provincial and republican officials balance a rhetoric emphasizing devolution with a desire to stem the flow of power past their own levels to the local organs of power. County officials vie for further devolution to their level, but often fail to support the final step of turning over power to the townships and obshchinas. All levels also balance the benefits of retaining powers with the costs (financial and other) of exerting this power responsibly.

BALANCING COMPETING AGENDAS

Evenkis must assess the tradeoffs of centralization of control over land versus its partial devolution, knowing that lower levels of government may meet fewer of their demands than the federal government. Historically, the federal government has provided minimal support. Yet in today's climate of privatization, Evenkis and other indigenous leaders look to other federal systems such as Canada and the United States, and see parallels. In these cases, if the federal governments have also failed to give much support to indigenous rights, they have at least protected indigenous peoples from even more callous treatment by provinces and states. Through an often negligent paternalism, the governments of Canada and the United States have still stemmed provincial and state initiatives which would have alienated indigenous lands much more rapidly than has happened under federal wardship. Similar scenarios are developing in the Russian North.

In several instances, Evenkis have supported federal initiatives as the best available in an unstable landscape of reform. Federal support for the transfer of land from crumbling state enterprises (e.g., sovkhozy) to obshchinas and protected areas in fact provides a politically astute means for the government to retain its control over land. Indigenous lands remain state lands. The alternative facing the government is loss of land to private individuals; the alternative facing Evenkis is the privatization of land and its subsequent sale by former *sovkhoz* administrators to the highest bidder. Ultimately, while Evenki and federal goals differ radically, the means to avoid such alternatives link Evenki interests with those of the federal government in an uneasy alliance. Each needs the other to stem privatization that will signify losses for both.

At the same time Evenkis pursue greater control over land in a political environment fraught with ethnic tensions, one that colors both federal and lower level reception of indigenous land rights initiatives. The move toward a more democratic society has for many Russians meant the move toward a society defined by equal rights (not equal opportunity, nor equitable rights) for all. Many Russian citizens feel that minority populations should not enjoy special rights, especially when they infringe on others' opportunities. Officials muster these concerns to deny indigenous rights. Witness the colorful exchange recounted regarding one petitioner's foiled attempt to gain an obshchina allotment, in which an Evenki's petition for land is analogized to armed confrontation in another part of the former Soviet Union:

> And Saganov came—he's our minister of Buryatia who deals with these [nationality] issues. [The petitioner for land] said, "That's where I hunted since childhood," so that they would given him the territory for the creation of an obshchina. But [Saganov] didn't give it to [the petitioner]. [Saganov] said, "you aren't going to create a second Nagorno–Karabakh here." (A. T., April 1994)

In this case, the petitioner had asked for ancestral land currently used by non-Evenki hunters; awarding his petition would have removed valuable hunting lands from non-Evenki usage. Saganov, the republican official, contextualized the allocation of such an obshchina allotment in graphic terms, comparing it to the war between the Armenians and Azerbayjans over the province of Nagorno–Karabakh. If exaggerating the possible outcome, Saganov's words emphasized both the tensions inherent in indigenous land claims, and the opportunities for exploiting these tensions to official purpose.

For related reasons, some Evenki individuals have applauded the approach taken by the Chita provincial government, which specifically avoided differentiating "Territories of Traditional Nature Use" along nationality lines, and underscored instead "professional" ones—such territories were created in order to protect the activities of *all* hunters and reindeer herders, Evenki or otherwise. In the rocky economic and political climate, these Evenkis accede that the primacy given indigenous peoples' rights will unlikely be great. The state will use indigenous rights as a politically opportune platform for international consumption and will trim its policies domestically to meet majority opinions. Chita's shift in the rhetoric surrounding land claims from indigenous rights to sustainable development may make the concept of both "Territories of Traditional Nature Use" and obshchina lands more palatable for many in Transbaykalia, a fact not ignored by a number of Evenkis. At the same time, in providing for sustainable economic development, such lands can also provide for sustainable cultural development for the Evenkis.

Yet sidestepping the issue of aboriginal rights to land, whether it be through the establishment of "de-ethnicized" Territories of Traditional Nature Use, the lack of guarantee for indigenous representation in "native" administrative units, or the allocation of use rights to, but not devolution of ownership of, obshchina lands, provides but a short-term solution to the Evenki predicament in northern Transbaykalia. In an increasingly legalized Russian society, this issue of land rights must sooner or later be confronted and resolved. Against the turmoil of reforms, seen in civil war, climbing crime rates, wage arrears, collapses in the delivery of critical supplies, the demands of a small number of indigenous persons living in remote areas quickly becomes lost. However, the Evenkis and other indigenous peoples may be able to use this "Time of Troubles" to forward their agendas.

Perhaps the greatest tool the Evenkis may now utilize in their pursuit for more fully developed land rights is the concomitant trends of legalization and internationalization of Russian society. The Russian Federation's Constitution explicitly recognizes and guarantees indigenous rights, as defined by the international conventions which most generously define these rights (Konstitutsiya 1993; §69). The Russian Federation, in need of international economic and political support, must show advances in protecting the legal rights of its citizens. Global concerns with indigenous rights, while still modest, have grown dramatically in the past decade. In this context, can the Evenkis employ such constitutional guarantees to further push the dimensions of land rights to meet their social, economic, and cultural needs? Can they depend on the international community to support them in doing so?

Glossary of Russian and Evenki Terms

Bamovtsy Persons who work on the building and servicing of the Baykal–Amur Railroad (BAM), mostly recent arrivals to Siberia ("BAM–ers").

Goskomsever State Committee of the Russian Federation on Questions of Development of the North. Among other mandates, it oversees issues pertaining to the indigenous population of the Russian Federation's northern regions.

gospromkhoz State hunting enterprise. This economic organization focuses mainly on hunting activities; its workers are salaried employees.

inorodtsy "Aliens," the term used for non-Russian inhabitants of the Russian Empire during the Tsarist period.

kolkhoz Collective farm. Under this form of economic organization, workers communally owned the assets of the farm and shared in profits made by the farm. Wages were dependent on producing a profit.

koopzverpromkhoz Cooperative Hunting Enterprise. Another form of economic organization, similar to a *gospromkhoz* but originally established along the collective economic principles of the *kolkhoz.*

labaz Elevated storage platform, used to cache food, clothing, and tools. Another form of labaz was built as a platform on which to deposit the bones of ritually sacrificed animals.

obshchina A small indigenous community, formerly kin-based, currently kin or non-kin based. Many ethnographers identify the obshchina as the basic social unit of most indigenous societies in the Russian North.

Orochëny "People of the Deer," a self-designation used by reindeer herding Evenkis of Northern Transbaykalia and neighboring areas. Singular: Orochën.

oron Domesticated reindeer (Evenki term).

Sakha A people of Turkic origin, who migrated to Central Siberia during the last millennium. Called Yakut until recently.

sovkhoz State farm. An economic form of organization in which the state owns all assets and employees are wage laborers.

tayga Boreal forest, consisting predominantly of coniferous species.

Tungus Pre-Soviet name for Evenkis (from Sakha, *Tongus*). This term is used by some Evenkis in Northern Transbaykalia to refer to steppe-dwelling, cattle-raising Evenki of Southern Transbaykalia.

yasak Tax paid, usually in the form of furs, by indigenous Siberians, seventeenth through nineteenth centuries.

Appendix I

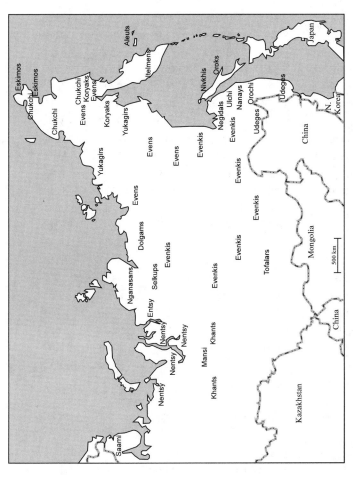

APPENDIX I Northern indigenous peoples of the Russian Federation.

135

NORTHERN INDIGENOUS PEOPLES OF THE RUSSIAN FEDERATION*

People	1926	1959	1970	1979	1989
Nentsy	13217	23007	28705	29894	34665
Evenkis	38805	24151	25471	27294	30163
Khants	17334	19410	21138	20934	22521
Evens	2044	9121	12029	12523	17199
Chukchi	12221	11727	13597	14000	15184
Nanays	5860	8026	10005	10516	12023
Koryaks	7439	6287	7487	7879	9242
Mansi	6095	6449	7710	7563	8474
Dolgans	656	3932	4877	5053	6945
Nivkhi	4076	3717	4420	4397	4673
Selkups	1630	3768	4282	3565	3612
Ulchi	723	2055	2448	2552	3233
Itelmens	859	1109	1301	1370	2481
Udegey	1357	1444	1469	1551	2011
Saami	1720	1792	1884	1888	1890
Eskimos	1293	1118	1308	1510	1719
Chuvans	705	na	na	na	1511
Nganasans	867	784	953	867	1278
Yukagirs	443	442	615	835	1142
Kets	1428	1019	1182	1122	1113
Orochi	647	782	1089	1198	915
Tofalars	413	586	620	763	731
Aleuts	353	421	451	546	702
Negidals	683	na	537	504	622
Entsy	482	na	na	na	209
Oroks	162	na	na	na	190
Total	121512	131111	153578	158324	184448

*Several other peoples (Alyutors, Kereks, Taz, Chulimtsy, Todzhas, Shors, Teleuts) were not included in previous censuses but are now being considered for inclusion as an official list of Numerically Small Peoples of the North.
na = data not available.
Sources: Gurvich 1987, p. 67; Pika and Prokhorov 1994, p. 195.

References

Abramov, I.
1930. "Economic activities of the Evenki population of the Tungiro–Olëkma County." *Taiga i Tundra* 2:13–15.

Abramova, G. V.
1991. "Legal status is needed." *Severyanka* (Newspaper of Tungiro–Olëkma County), 24 July 1991.

Alekseev, M. L., and A. K. Tulokhonov, eds.
1993. *Sever Buryatii [The North of Buryatia]*, Ulan–Ude: Buryatskiy Nauchnyy Tsentr SO RAN.

Anderson, B.
1983. *Imagined Communities. Reflections on the Origin and Spread of Nationalism*, revised edition. London: Verso.

Anderson, D. G.
1995. "National identity and belonging in Arctic Siberia. An ethnography of Evenkis and Dolgans at Khantaiskoe Ozero in the Taimyr Autonomous District." Ph.D. Dissertation, University of Cambridge.
1992. "Property rights and civil society in Siberia: An analysis of the social movements of the Zabaikal'skie Evenki." *Praxis Interntational* 12(1):83–105.
1991. "Turning hunters into herders: A critical examination of Soviet development policy among the Evenki of Southeastern Siberia." *Arctic* 44(1):12–22.

Aruneev, G.
1992. [No title recorded.] *Sovetskiy Sever* (Newspaper of Tungiro–Olëkma County), 27 February 1992.
1989. "Reindeer husbandry is being renewed." *Sovetskiy Sever* (Newspaper of Tungiro-Olëkma County), 4 April 1989.

Atlas Zabaykal'ya
1967. *Atlas Zabaykal'ya [Atlas of Transbaykalia]*. Irkutsk: Institut Geografii Sibiri i Dal'nego Vostoka.

Aypin, Ye.
1989. "Not by oil alone." *Moskovskie Novosti* 8 January 1989 (Translated into English in *Moscow News*, no. 2, 1989).

Baldunikov, A. I.
1936. "Non-hunting economic occupations of the Tungiro–Olëkma Evenkis," *Izvestiya Obshchestva Izucheniya Vostochno-Sibirskogo Kraya* 1(LVI):183–211.

Belikov, V., and E. Golubev
1991. "Conditions of labor and life of the Evenkis of Transbaykalia." *Vitimskie Zory* (Newspaper of Baunt County), 29 June 1991.

Bond, A.
1996. "The Russian copper industry and the Norl'sk Joint-Stock Company in the Mid-1990s." *Post-Soviet Geography and Economics* 37(5):286–329.

Boyko, V. I.
1979. *BAM i Narody Severa [BAM and the Peoples of the North]*. Novosibirsk: Nauka.

Butz, D.
1996. "Sustaining indigenous communities: Symoblic and instrumental dimensions of pastoral resource use in Shimshal, Northern Pakistan." *Canadian Geographer* 40(1):36–53.

Chekundaev, G.
1990. "Where my ancestors live." *Vitimskie Zory* (Newspaper of Baunt County), 18 August 1990.

Chunavlev, V.
1988. "First steps of the Baunt Young Communist League." *Vitimskie Zory* (Newspaper of Baunt County), 18 October 1988.

Conquest, R.
1986. *The Harvest of Sorrow. Soviet Collectivization and the Terror-Famine*. New York: Oxford University Press.

Dmitriev, V. S., K. B. Klokov, and M. M. Sorokina
1990. *Zashchita Interesov i Sovershenstvovanie Organizatsii Khozyaystvennoy Deyatel'nosti Korennogo Naseleniya Severa. Rekomendatsii [Defending the Interests and Improving the Organization of Economic Activities of the Indigenous Population of the North. Recommendations]*. Leningrad-Pushkin:

Nauchno-Isseldovatel'skiy Institut Ekonoimki i Organizatsii Sel'skokhozyzstvennogo Proizvodstva Nechernozemnoy Zony RSFSR.

Draft Law
n.d   Draft Law of the Russian Federation. Foundations of the Legal Status of Indigenous Peoples of the Russian North. Typescript.

Fondahl, G.
1996.   "Contested terrain: Changing boundaries and identities in Southeastern Siberia." *Post-Soviet Geography and Economics* 37(1):3–15.
1995.   "Legacies of territorial reorganization for indigenous land claims in Northern Russia." *Polar Geography and Geology* 19(1):1–21.

Forsyth, J.
1992.   *A History of the Peoples Of Siberia. Russia's North Asian Colony 1581–1990.* Cambridge: Cambridge University Press.

Gilev, A.
1934.   "Zametki o Bauntovskom rayone." *Sovetskiy Sever* 4:87–93.

Glazirova, M. S.
1990.   "Interview with M. S. Glazirova." *Severyanka* (Newspaper of Tungiro–Olyokma County), 17 Nov 1990.

Grant, B.
1995.   *In the House of Soviet Culture. A Century of Perestroikas.* Princeton: Princeton University Press.

Grigoreva, M. F.
1992.   "Homelands—to their owners." *Vitimskie Zory* (Newspaper of Baunt County), 26 September 1992.

Grigorovskiy, N. M.
1890.   "Trip on the Verkhne Angara." *Izvestiya Vostochno-Sibirskogo otdela Rossiyskogo Geograficheskogo Obshchestva* 23(2):1–29.

Gubel'man, M. I.
1925.   "On the Tungus of the Olëkminsk District (from travel notes of a trip along the Olëkma River in the summer of 1916)." *Izvestiya Gosudarstvennogo Rossiyskogo Geograficheskogo Obshchestva* 52(2):33–51.

Gurvich, I. S., ed.
1987.   *Etnicheskoe razvitie narodnostei Severa v sovetskiy period [Ethnic Development of the nationalities of the North in the Soviet Period].* Moscow: Nauka.

Ingold, T.
1980. *Hunters, Pastoralists and Ranchers. Reindeer Economies and Their Transformations.* Cambridge: Cambridge University Press.

Iz Bauntovskogo
1935. From Baunt County. *Sovetskiy Sever* 1:104–105.

Kaiser, R.
1994. *The Geography of Nationalism in Russia and the USSR.* Princeton: Princeton University Press.

Klobukov, B.
n.d. Ekonomicheskoy Ocherk Bauntovskogo rayona B.-M. A. S. S. R. Ekspeditiya Burnarkomzema [Economic Report on the Baunt County of the B.-M. A. S. S. R. Expedition of Buryat People's Committee on Land]. Volume 2. (Typescript archived at the Museum of the Peoples of the North, Bagdarin, Baunt County.)

Knapp, G.
1992. *The Population of the Circumpolar North.* Anchorage: Institute of Social and Economic Research, University of Alaska.

Kolesnikov, M. A.
1983. "Orientation of Evenkis of the North of the Irkutsk Province to traditional and non-traditional types of employment." In: *Narodnosti Severa: Problemy i Perspektivy Economicheskogo i Sotsial'nogo Razvitiya,* 17–20. Novosibirsk.

Konstitutsiya
1993. *Konstitutsiya Rossiyskoy Federatsii, prinyata vsenarodnym golosovaniem 12 dekabrya 1993 g. [Constitution of the Russian Federation, Adopted by a Nationwide Plebiscite, 12 December 1993].* Moscow: Yuridicheskaya Literatura.

Kozulin, V. N.
1991. *Baunt (Proshloe i Nastoyashchee) [Baunt (Past and Present)].* Bagdarin: Musuem of the Peoples of the North of Buryatia.

Krupnik, I.
1993. *Arctic Adaptations.Native Whalers and Reindeer Herders of Northern Eurasia.* Hanover, N. H.: University Press of New England.

Kryazhkov, V., ed.
1994. *Status malochislennykh Narodov Rossiya. Pravovye Akty i Dokumenty.* Moscow: Yuridicheskaya Literatura.

Kryukov, I. F.
1908. *Otchet Proizvoditelya Rabot I. F. Kryukova o Komandirovke v Barguzinskuyu Taygu Zabaykal'skoy Oblasti v 1905 g. dlya Issledovaniya ee v Kolonizatsionnom Otnoshenii [Report of the Superintendent of Works. I. F. Kryukov on ta Trip to the Barguzin Tayga of the Zabaykal Province in 1905].* Irkutsk: Izdanie Amurskoy partii po obrazovaniyu pereselenshceskikh uchastkov v Zabaykal'skoy oblasti.

Lorgoktoev, V.
1992. "Renewal by actions, not by words." *Vitimskie Zory* (Newspaper of Baunt County), 13 February 1992.

Martin, J.
1986. *Treasure of the Land of Darkness. The Fur Trade and Its Significance for Medieval Russia.* Cambridge: Cambridge University Press.

Materialy
1990. *Materialy s"ezda malochislennykh narodov Severa [Materials from the Congress of the Numerically Small Peoples of the North].* Moscow.

Mazholis, G. M., M. B. Vachelenova, A. A. Ganyugina, V. A. Ganyugin, V. G. Anikin, A. B. Meshkov, and V. S. Platanov
1994. Protocol of the meeting of hunters having allotments along the Chaya River Valley. Document filed with the Association of Numerically Small Peoples of the North of the Severo–Baykal County, 11 April 1994.

Mikheev, V. S., ed.
1995. *Traditsionnoe Prirodopol'zovanie Evenkov. Obosnovanie Territoriy v Chitinskoy Oblasti [Traditional Nature Use of the Evenkis. Bases for Territory in the Chita Province].* Novosibirsk: Nauka.

Mordvinov, A.
1851. "The Orochens or Reindeer Tungus." *Sovremennik* 6:126–135.

Murashko, O.
1996. "Legal status of the indigenous Numerically Small Peoples of Russia." *Zhivaya Arktika* 3:11–12.

Nemtushkin, A.
1988a. "My pain, Evenkia." *Sovetskaya Kul'tura* 29 July 1988.
1988b. "Should mistakes be multiplied?" *Sotsialisticheskaya Industriya,* 28 June 1988.

Neupokoev, V.
1928. *Tungusy Buryatii (Ocherk) [The Tungus of Buryatia (Notes)].* Verkhneudinsk: Zhizn' Buryatii.

Nietschmann, B.
1994. "The Fourth World: Nations vs. states." In: *Reordering the World. Geopolitical Perspectives on the 21st Century.* G. Demko and W. B. Wood (eds.), 225–242. Boulder: Westview.

Nikul'shin, N. P.
1939. *Pervobytnye Proizvodstvennye Ob"edineniya i Sotsialisticheskoe Stroitel'stvo u Evenkov [Primitive Production Unions and Socialist Construction Among the Evenkis].* Leningrad: Izdatel'stvo Glavsevmorputi.

O neotlozhnykh
1992. O neotlozhnykh merakh po zashchite mest prozhivaniya i khozyaystvennoy deyatel'nosti malochislennykh narodov Severa [On Urgent Measures for the Protection of the Places of Residence and Economic Activity of the Numerically Small Peoples of the North]. *Ukaz Prezidenta Rossiyskoy Federatsii no. 397,* April 22, 1992.

O svobodnom
1990. O svobodnom natsional'nom razvitii grazhdan SSSR, prozhivayushchikh za predelami svoikh natsioal'nykh gosudarstvennykh obrazovaniy ili ne imeyushchikh na territorii SSSR (On the Free National Development of Citizens of the USSR, Living Beyond the Boundariea of Their National State Formations or Not Possessing Such in the Territory in the USSR). *Zakon SSSR,* April 26, 1990.

Ob obrazovanii
1991. Ob obrazovanii na territorii Buryatskoy SSR evenkiyskikh sel'skikh Sovetov narodnykh deputatov [On the Formation of Evenki Rural Councils of People's Deputies on the Territory of the Buryat SSR]. Postanovlenie Verkhovnogo Soveta Buryatskoy Sovetskoy Sotsialisticheskoy Respubliki, 17 January 1991. *Vedomosti Verkhovnogo Soveta Respubliki Buryatii* 2:61–62.

Orlov
1858. Baunt and Angara Wandering Tungus. *Vestnik Imperatskogo Russkogo Geograficheskogo Obshchestva,* Part 21 (St. Petersburg), 180–192.

Osherenko, G.
1995. "Property rights and transformation in Russia: Institutional change in the Far North." *Europe-Asia Studies* 47(7): 1077–1108.

Partinye
1980. *Partinye organizatsii Sovetskogo Severa (1920–1959 gg.) [Party Organization in the Soviet North (1920–1959)].* Part 1. Tomsk: Izdatel'stvo Tomskogo universiteta.

Pika, A. I., and B. B. Prokhorov
1988. "The big problems of the Small Peoples," *Kommunist* 16: 76–83. (Translated into English: "Soviet Union: The big problems of small ethnic groups, *IWGIA Newsletter* 57: 123–135.)

Pika, A. I., and B. B. Prokhorov, eds.
1994. *Neotraditsionalizm na Rossiyskom Severe [Neotraditionalisn in the Russian North].* Moscow.

Poelzer, G.
1996. "Toward a theory of native self-government: Canada and Russia in comparative perspective." Ph.D. Thesis, University of Alberta.

Pomishin, S. B.
1990. *Proiskhozhdenie Olenevodstva i Domestikatsiya Severnogo Olenya [The Origins and Reindeer Husbandry and the Domestication of the Reindeer].* Moscow: Nauka.

Rytkheu, Yu.
1988. "Slogans and amulets." *Komsomolskaya Pravda,* 19 May 1988.

Sangi, V.
1988. "Alienation." *Sovetskaya Rossiya,* 11 November 1988.

Savin, M.
1989. "How I came to school." *Vitimskie Zory* (Newspaper of Baunt County), 16 March 1989.

Schindler, D.
1996. *Indigenous Peoples and Development in the Chukchi Autonomous Okrug.* INSROP Working Paper No. 51–1996, IV.4.1.

Sergeev, M. A.
1955. *Nekapitalisitcheskiy put' razvitiya malykh narodov Severa [The Non-capitalist Path of Development of the Small Peoples of the North].*Trudy AN Instituta Etnografii, NS, Volume 27.

Shirokogoroff, S. M.
1966. *Social Organization of the Northern Tungus.* Shanghai: The Commercial Press. (First published in 1929)

Shubin, A. S.
1967. Evenki Severa Buryatskoy ASSR (Istoriko-etnograficheskie ocherki) [Evenkis of the North of the Buryat ASSR (Historical-ethnografical Notes)]. Candidate Dissertation, N. N. Miklukho-Maklaya Institute of Ethnography, Academy of Sciences of the USSR.

Sirina, A. A.
1995. Katangskie Evenki v XXv. Rasselenie, Organizatsiya Sredy Zhiznedeyatel'nosti [Katanga Evenkis in the 20th Century. Distribution, Organization of the Subsistence Environment]. Moscow: Institut etnologii i Atropologii im. N. N. Miklykho-Maklaya RAN.
1992a. "Continuity in the organization of the subsistence environment" (the example of the Evenkis of the Upper Nizhnaya Tunguska River). Etnograficheskoe Obozrenie 2:77–89.
1992b. Rasselenie i Organizatsii Sredi Zhiznedeyatel'nosti u Evenkov (verkhov'ya r. Nizhnaya Tunguska XX v.) [Distribution and Organization of the Evenki Subsistence Environment (Upper Reaches of the Nizhnaya Tunguska River). Abstract of Candidate Dissertation, N. N. Miklukho-Maklaya Institute of Ethnology and Anthropology, Russian Academy of Sciences. Moscow.

Slezkine, Yu.
1994. Arctic Mirrors. Russia and the Small Peoples of the North. Ithaca, N.Y.: Cornell University Press.

Snegur, A.
1993. "Conflict at the Fairytale Mountains." Zabaykal'skiy Rabochiy, 19 August 1993.
1989. "Where are the Evenkis headed? Notes on the problems of the indigenous population of the Kalar County," Zabaykal'skiy Rabochiy, 19 January 1989.

Solovova, A. T.
1993. On the issue of political administrative division in multiethnic regions. Typescript for Zapiski Zabaykal'skogo filiala Russkogo Geograficheskogo Obshchestva, Volume 128, Chita.

Sovetskiy Sever   (Newspaper of the Tungokochen County)

State Duma of the Federal Assembly of the Russian Federation, Committee on Nationalities
1995. Acts and Other Legislative Standards Relating to the Political and Socio-Economic Development of the Indigenous Peoples of Russia (19th–20th centuries). Self-

Governmeent, Land and Natural Resources. A Comparative Analysis and Outlook. Report to the International Conference to Assist Russian Federal Programmes Supporting Aboriginal Peoples of the North. Moscow. (Typescript)

Strakach, Yu. B.
1962. "On the issue of productive traditions among the Evenkis." *Kratkie Soobshcheniya Instituta Etnografii* 37:46–56.

Stremilov, P. I.
1970. "Prospects for the development of agriculture, reindeer husbandry and hunting on the kolkhozy of the Northern Counties of the Chita Province." In: *Voprosy proizvodstvennogo okhotovedeniya Sibiri i Dal'nego Vostoka,* 228–235. Irkutsk.

Sytin, V.
1929. "The Angara in Haze." *Okhotnik Sibiri* 1:21–22.

Tugolukov, V. I.
1980. *Idushie Poperek Khrebtov.* Krasnoyarsk: Krasnoyarskoe knizhnoe izdatel'stvo.
1962. "The Vitimo-Olëkma Evenkis." *Sibirskiy Etnograficheskiy Sbornik* 4:67–97.

Tugolukov, V. I., and A. S. Shubin
1969. "Collective farm construction among the Evenkis of Northern Buryatia and its influence on their lifeways and culture." *Etnograficheskiy Sbornik* (Ulan-Ude) 5:42–64.

Turov, M. G.
1990. *Khozyaystvo Evenkov Taezhnoy Zony Sredney Sibiri v Kontse XIX-Nachale XX V. [Economy of the Evenkis of the Tayga Zone of Central Siberia at the End of the 19th and Beginning of the 20th Centuries].* Irkutsk: Izdatel'stvo Irkutskogo Universiteta.

V Baykitskom
1934. "In the Baykit and Chuna Counties of the Evenki National District (some data on the basis of land use)." *Sovetskiy Sever* 2:99–100.

Vasilevich, G. M.
1969. *Evenki. Istoriko-etnograficheskie Ocherki (XVIII-Nachale XX v.) [Evenkis Historical-Ethnographical Notes (17th-Beginning of 20th Century].* Leningrad: Nauka.
1930. "The Vitim-Tungiro-Olëkma Tungus." *Sovetskiy Sever* 3:96–113.

Vasilevich, G. M., and A. V. Smolyak
1964. "The Evenkis." In: *The Peoples of Siberia*. M. G. Levin and L. P. Potapov (eds.), 620–654. Chicago: University of Chicago Press.

Vakhtin, N. B.
1994. "Native peoples of the Russian Far North." In: *Polar Peoples. Self-Determination and Development*. Minority Rights Group (eds.), 29–80. London: Minority Rights Group.

Voronin, A.
1932. "A short economic overview of the Severo–Baykal County," *Sovetskiy Sever* 1–2:188–195.

Voskoboynikov, M. G.
1961. "Some data on the ethnography of the Evenkis of Buryatia." *Etnograficheskiy Sbornik* 2:29–42.

Zibarev, V. A.
1968. *Sovetskoe Stroitel'stvo u Malykh Narodnostey Severa (1917–1932 gg.) [Soviet Construction among the Small Peoples of the North (1917–1932)]*. Tomsk.

Zisser, V.
1929. "Wandering Tungus of the Chara Uplands." *Okhotnik i Rybak Sibiri* 3:50–52.

Zuev, Yu. N.
1984. "To raise the quality of furs." *Sovetskiy Sever* (Newspaper of Tungiro–Olëkma County), 31 March 1994.

Archival Resources

GAChO   Gosudarstvennyy Arkhiv Chitinskoy Oblasti (State Archive of the Chita Province), Chita.

LOZ   Letopis ot Zarechnoe (Chronicles from Zarechnoe) Community archive maintained at the Zarechnoe Rural Library, Tungiro–Olëkma County.

TsGAOR   Tsentral'nyy Gosudarstvennyy Arkhiv Oktyabrskoy Revolyutsii (Central State Archive of the October Revolution) [Now part of the Gosdarstvennyy Arkhiv Rossiyskoy Federatsii], Moscow.